Maximum Risk

True Adventures
of a
Homeland Security Pilot

Rocky Anderson

iUniverse, Inc.
Bloomington

Maximum Risk
True Adventures of a Homeland Security Pilot

iUniverse books may be ordered through booksellers or by contacting:

iUniverse
1663 Liberty Drive
Bloomington, IN 47403
www.iuniverse.com
1-800-Authors (1-800-288-4677)

Because of the dynamic nature of the Internet, any web addresses or links contained in this book may have changed since publication and may no longer be valid.

Any people depicted in stock imagery provided by Thinkstock are models, and such images are being used for illustrative purposes only.

Certain stock imagery © Thinkstock.

ISBN: 978-1-4502-8994-8 (sc)
ISBN: 978-1-4502-8995-5 (ebk)

Printed in the United States of America

iUniverse rev. date: 2/2/2011

DEDICATION

For my wife, Lee Ann, and my children, Tommy, Adam, and Megan.
They sacrificed a great deal while I was off flying around the world.

INTRODUCTION

For more than twenty-three years, I chased drug smugglers and terrorists across a dozen different countries, flying a wide variety of government airplanes and helicopters for the world's largest law enforcement air force. Since I was a pilot, I kept a logbook of all my flights, making notes if anything out of the ordinary happened. It often did. This book is a true account of some of my most exciting adventures, working some of the United States' biggest drug cases, protecting the president of the United States, and going undercover against major drug lords.

I will describe my visits to exotic islands in the Caribbean, the jungles of South America, the deserts of northern Mexico, the swamps of Louisiana, and working the southern border of the United States. You will get my impressions of the US presidents, congressmen, movie stars, and heads of major drug cartels that I have met along the way.

In no way am I speaking for or representing the United States Department of Homeland Security in any capacity in this book. I tell these stories from my personal perspective, as truthfully and as accurately as possible—without revealing any classified information. The tales are not watered-down nor politically correct. For good or bad, I tell them as they happened.

These flights and cases involved a great deal of help from other pilots, agents, mechanics, and a host of other ground support people. It was a team effort, not a one man show. Out of regard for their security, none of their names were mentioned.

CHAPTER ONE

The view was surreal from the cockpit of the Homeland Security jet interceptor I was flying. I was assigned airspace security duty over the most important group of people in the United States and possibly the world. It was President George W. Bush's second inauguration, and I was circling Washington, D.C. at 7,000 feet. It was a beautiful day, and I could see a crowd of nearly100,000 people below, which included the president of the United States, two former presidents, most of Congress, the Supreme Court, and many other national and international VIPs. Millions of people around the world were watching the event on TV. It was one of those rare moments in life when you find yourself involved in something much bigger than you ever could have imagined. My only prayer was, "Lord, don't let me screw up!"

I could see the White House, the Capitol building, the Washington Monument, and all the other sites of Washington, D.C. from a perspective that few people have ever had. High above me were two F-16 fighter jets, and below me were batteries of surface-to-air missiles set strategically around the city. Two of Homeland Security's Blackhawk helicopters were circling five miles to the north and south. There were other protective measures in place that I'm not going to discuss for security reasons. The tragedy of 9/11 was still fresh in everyone's mind, and no one was taking any chances on security. Along with the usual threats, a very disturbing one had developed. Two days earlier, someone had stolen a stealth ultralight aircraft from a nearby military base. This aircraft, used by special force units, was almost invisible to radar, and its theft had us all concerned about the day's event.

To protect the airspace, we set up a three-layer approach, which some referred to as a "sandwich." With fighters armed with missiles above me and surface-to-air missiles below me, I felt like the bologna in the middle of a sandwich. That's because my aircraft had no weapons aboard, except for the pistols that we had in our shoulder holsters. If the ultralight got through the outer rings of security, about the best we could do with our aircraft was to ram it. Because it was very light, if we could clip it with our wingtip, we could destroy it with only minor damage to our aircraft. At least, that's what we hoped.

My part of the mission was not only to watch for this ultralight but to intercept and identify any other slow-moving aircraft that entered the thirty-mile restricted ring of airspace around Washington, D.C. Numerous times since 9/11, when this restricted airspace was put in place, small general aviation type aircraft had accidentally violated the airspace and caused the evacuation of the White House and the Capitol building. This not only created a major disruption to government business, it generated panic among the people having to evacuate. The frequency of these evacuations ultimately led to a decision: the Department of Homeland Security's US Customs and Border Protection (CBP) was placed in charge of airspace security over D.C. The area became known as the National Capital Region (NCR).

The Office of Air and Marine is a part of US Customs and Border Protection. With more than three hundred aircraft and two hundred boats, the Office of Air and Marine is the largest law enforcement air and maritime force in the world. Not only were all the pilots federal agents, they also flew the perfect aircraft for this mission—CBP's jet interceptor, the Cessna Citation II, is a highly modified business jet. This aircraft can fly over four hundred miles per hour at top speed, yet it can still fly slowly enough to intercept and track the slowest of most general aviation aircraft. The pilots were already highly skilled in intercepting these types of aircraft because they had been chasing drug smugglers for years.

CBP also had several Blackhawk helicopters in their inventory. Also piloted by pilot/federal agents, the Blackhawks were perfect for landing at the small airports used by general aviation aircraft and conducting searches and arrests. That was something the military could not do, due to the Posse Comitatus Act that prevents the military from making arrests.

The air force would still handle fast-moving aircraft, but CBP would first intercept and identify all the targets flying under two hundred miles per hour entering the restricted airspace. Most of the airspace incursions were small, slow-moving, general aviation aircraft. There are several small airports surrounding the Washington, D.C. area, with lots of small plane traffic. The restricted airspace was put in place around D.C. so quickly that it was over a year before it was even depicted on aviation charts. As a result, many of the airspace violations occurred simply because the pilots were confused about the new restrictions.

I had intercepted one such confused pilot only a month before. I was on the alert crew at Reagan Washington National Airport (DCA) when we got the call to scramble on an unidentified target entering the NCR. I jumped into our jet and began taxiing out, only to find the taxiways crowded with airliners waiting in line to take off. Since we had priority, the control tower held all the airliners in place. I was able to weave between them to the runway. I remember that, at one point, one of my wings slid under the wing of a large airliner. Despite the heavy airline traffic on the ground, I was able to get airborne within the eight-minute scramble window.

Minutes later, I had the target locked up on the air-to-air radar, the same radar used in F-16 fighters. I rolled out of my turn one mile in trail of the target. I quickly brought back the power and lowered the flaps and landing gear to slow down. The target was a small, single-engine airplane that was flying very slowly, but I managed to slow down enough to pull up beside it and fly in formation only two wing spans away. On the nose of my jet was painted in large letters, "POLICE 121.5." The number 121.5 represents the universal aviation emergency frequency. I rocked my wings to get the pilot's attention. I can still remember the look on the pilot's face when he turned and saw my jet flying only feet away. His eyes were as large as silver dollars. I remember hoping that he was not so frightened that he would do something stupid like turn into my airplane.

Luckily, the pilot changed his radio to the proper frequency and we were able to talk to him. It turned out that he was simply lost. We were able to get him to turn around, and we guided him to a nearby airport that was just outside the thirty-mile circle. One of our Blackhawk helicopters, which had also been scrambled, landed behind him, and the agents gave him a lesson in navigation I'm sure he will never forget. The agents said he was so nervous that they were worried that he was going to have a heart attack. I always wondered how he would feel if he knew that he had been only minutes away from being shot down.

After many other intercepts like this one, we began to worry that an innocent aircraft might be accidentally shot down. Then it almost happened. A fighter jet came within seconds of shooting down the governor of Kentucky. The governor was flying into the D.C. area from Kentucky when, about a hundred miles from D.C., his plane's transponder malfunctioned. A transponder is a device that sends out a radar code so that air traffic controllers on the ground can identify the aircraft. It is required for all flights into the D.C. area. The pilot of the governor's airplane notified air traffic controllers of the problem before entering the restricted airspace and was told that the plane could continue to its destination—Reagan Washington National Airport. However, the air traffic controller failed to pass on this information to the next controller, who was actually in charge of the restricted airspace. That controller scrambled an air force fighter when he saw an aircraft he could not identify, without a transponder code, heading straight for the heart of Washington, D.C. Minutes later, the fighter jet was closing in on the governor's airplane with a "green light" to shoot the aircraft down.

The only thing that saved the governor from being shot down was the weather. It was a cloudy day, and the air force pilot was having a hard time getting a good visual on the aircraft (required by the rules of engagement) in order shoot it down with his aircraft's Gatling guns. It took several passes before the fighter finally got a good lock on the aircraft. Seconds before the air force pilot would have pulled the trigger, the FAA discovered its mistake and called off the fighter.

That was not the only time that we had trouble with the FAA controllers. We began doing routine patrols circling the D.C. area in our Citations. This created a lot of extra work for the FAA. In making a twenty-mile circle around D.C., we often had to talk to as many as five different controllers. They quickly grew tired of continually handing us off to one controller after another. This friction culminated one day when I was ferrying a Citation from New Orleans up to the Reagan Washington National Airport (DCA). Before I had taken off, I had received a call from our command center in D.C. telling me that the FAA now required all aircraft entering the thirty-mile ring around D.C. to have a code word. He gave me the code word, and I was set to go. What he did not tell me was that the code word was supposed to be used discreetly at a certain point in the normal communication with air traffic control on entering the area.

The flight was normal until we contacted approach control just before entering the thirty-mile restricted area. The FAA controller instructed us to land at the Dulles Airport, not our intended destination. Now, we were using the call sign of a Homeland Security aircraft, so the controller had to know who we were. We got back on the radio and told him our destination was DCA. On another radio, we contacted our office at DCA and instructed them to call approach control on the telephone and explain who we were. We tried giving him the password, but it was too late—we hadn't given it to him at the proper time. Even after all this, the controller still insisted we land at Dulles. This was no place for an argument, so I flew the plane to Dulles and landed.

While I was taxiing in at Dulles, the ground controller directed us away from the terminal to a remote spot on the airport grounds. As we were taxiing, we were suddenly joined by several police vehicles and escorted in. The jet I was flying had Homeland Security written in big letters on both sides, and the Homeland Security seal was on the tail. As soon as we parked, armed airport security surrounded the plane. Since everyone in the aircraft was armed and we did not want to get into a blue-on-blue situation, meaning cop against cop, we stayed in the aircraft until we called our office and had them call Dulles Airport Security to make sure they knew we were the good guys. After that was done, the tension relaxed and we got out of the airplane. We were all in flight suits and clearly identified as federal agents. Airport security got a big laugh out of the whole incident. I called the FAA and talked to a supervisor, and we were soon on our way to DCA. After that event, CBP management met with FAA management and worked out our problems. Soon we were once again one big, happy family.

President Bush finally ended his speech, and I landed back at Reagan National Airport, thankful that nothing had happened and the security mission had been a success. It had been a great day, and the best part of it all was that I hadn't screwed up!

This was actually the second big event for which I had flown security in the past year. I was also overhead in D.C. during the dedication of the World War II Memorial. On that occasion, I had the opportunity to shake hands with former presidents Bush and Clinton, whose aircraft were parked next to mine. During my dozen or so tours of duty working in D.C., I met many of our government leaders: the attorney general, the directors of the FBI, FAA, and DEA, and several congressmen. Former President George Bush was the one most of us pilots liked the best. He is one of the nicest people I've ever met. Every time he flew in, he made a point of stopping by to visit us and thank us for the job we were doing. I guess that, since he was a former pilot, he just naturally bonded with us pilots. He is truly a class act.

I later saw his son President George W. Bush during his visit to McAllen, Texas. He walked right beside me and made eye contact, but there were so many people around that I didn't get a chance to shake his hand.

Former President Clinton would come in, especially if there was a female around, but in my opinion, he was not as friendly as Bush. Once, when Clinton was taking pictures with us, one of our pilots put a cigar in his sleeve pin pocket and stood beside Clinton, making sure to get the cigar in the shot. He was very proud of that picture. Clinton's secret service agent just shook his head. I later flew with a pilot in Iraq who had flown Clinton in Marine One, the big helicopter you often see landing on the White House lawn. He said that Clinton was actually very friendly and pretty cool when he was relaxed at Camp David.

The inauguration was one of the special days to remember in my twenty-three-year career as a pilot and agent with Homeland Security and legacy US Customs Service. But there have been many of these special days, for I had what I considered the best job in the world. The US government had given me the opportunity to fly airplanes and helicopters on exciting missions throughout the United States and in a dozen other countries. I have met three US presidents, numerous congressmen, commissioners, state governors, movie stars, county sheriffs, police chiefs, and a host of other fascinating people. I've worked with many foreign embassy personnel as well as high-ranking military and government officials from other countries. I've had the chance to work on interesting criminal investigations and experienced the thrill of working undercover cases in several different countries. I still can't believe that I was getting paid to have so much fun.

CHAPTER TWO

I was raised in rural Tennessee and learned to fly there out of a small airport, thanks to the benefits of the GI Bill. At that time, the GI Bill paid 90 percent of the cost of flight training. I had volunteered to go to Vietnam soon after high school, but the war ended while I was still in military police training, so I ended up serving my two years in the army at Ft. Ord, California.

I could lie to you and tell you I volunteered for patriotic reasons, but the truth is I joined the military for three reasons: The first reason was that I had never ridden on a Greyhound bus, and that's how they transported us to basic training. Second, they issued us each two new pairs of boots. Third, I knew that the benefits from the GI Bill would be the only way I would ever be able to afford college or flight training.

I was a pilot for over ten years before I ever knew that the US Customs Service even had airplanes. The only thing I knew about customs was that they were the ones who searched your luggage when you entered the country. I was reading a magazine one day, and it had an article about how US Customs used airplanes and helicopters to chase drug smugglers. It sounded like a fantastic job. You got to fly airplanes and helicopters and carry a gun. They were looking for pilots, but according to the article, they only hired dual-rated pilots, meaning pilots who can fly both airplanes and helicopters. Apparently, these types of experienced pilots were in short supply. Customs was also looking for pilots who had law enforcement backgrounds.

The job sounded perfect for me. I had airline transport pilot certificates—the highest ratings given by the FAA—in both airplanes and helicopters. I also had flight instructor certificates in airplanes and helicopters. In addition, I had been a military policeman. But hold on, I had to think about this a little more. I owned a successful helicopter flight school, in which I taught people from around the world to fly helicopters. Taking this job would mean selling off my company and moving to somewhere along the border. It would be a big change. I was bored with instructing and this job sounded exciting, but I still shouldn't rush into this kind of a major decision, I told myself.

I waited a full five minutes before deciding to apply for the job. Unfortunately, the magazine article gave no clue as to how to apply. I picked up the phone and called the operator and asked for a number in Washington, D.C. for the US Customs Service. I was transferred to several people before I finally reached someone who said they would send me an application. Within days, I had received the application, filled it out, and mailed it in. Two weeks later, I received a call from the New Orleans Air Branch. The caller only asked me one question: "Do you really have eighteen hundred hours flying an R22 helicopter?"

The Robinson R22 helicopter was the small training helicopter that I operated in my helicopter flight school. It was a great little helicopter, used mostly for flight training. It was relatively new on the market and had some very unusual flight characteristics. Most helicopter flight instructors were not yet acquainted with these characteristics, which led to a large number of helicopter training accidents. Unfortunately, the R22 had gotten the reputation of being a very dangerous and difficult helicopter to fly.

So when I answered that I did indeed have eighteen hundred hours of flight time in an R22, I immediately got the job. I was told there was no need to come down for an interview, that my paperwork would be processed, and I would be told when to report to work. I later asked why I was hired without an interview or a flight check ,and I was told that anyone who could survive eighteen hundred hours in an R22 was either the best pilot in the world or the luckiest. Either way they wanted me!

Thinking back on the years I flew the Robinson R22, it *is* a wonder I did survive. I had bought seven R22s over the three-year period that I owned and operated Mid South Helicopters. I would buy a helicopter with low flight time, fly it for approximately five hundred hours, and then resell it. At that time, R22s were appreciating in value so quickly that I was able to sell the helicopters for more than I paid for them. Therefore, I was basically flying the five hundred hours for free, except of course for fuel, maintenance, and insurance. It was a good business.

Due to my flight school and others like it, word quickly got out around the world that the R22 was an economical flight training helicopter. One day, two gentlemen from England arrived at my office. They wanted to buy one of my helicopters and ship it to England to start a flight school. We made the deal, and soon afterward, they started what was to become the largest helicopter flight school in Europe. I also sold two helicopters to a company in New Zealand; that helped introduce R22s to that part of the world. We took the rotor blades off and managed to ship the two helicopters to New Zealand on a regular, airline DC-10 aircraft.

I had students in my flight school from England, Germany, Spain, Greece, South Africa, Australia, and various other countries. Many of them had plans to start helicopter companies back in their home countries. I had many interesting offers to go help set up these companies, but at that time in my life I had other plans and commitments.

But getting back to me surviving eighteen hundred hours in an R22, I would like to think that I survived on my superior skill and intellect, but I know better. I survived by the grace of God. I recall one flight with a student from Nigeria whom I was teaching to do autorotations. This is a maneuver that allows you to safely land the helicopter in the event of an engine failure in flight. With the possible exception of a night landing on an aircraft carrier, this is probably the most dangerous, demanding, and frightening maneuver in aviation.

In training, you begin the maneuver by cutting the power to idle, simulating an engine failure. The next step is to immediately lower the collective, which changes the pitch of the rotor blades so that they keep spinning while the helicopter is descending. By the way, when a helicopter loses its power, it falls out of the sky like a greased brick. It's extremely important to keep the rotor blades turning a certain RPM so that when you get just above the ground, you can use that momentum to cushion the landing. In an R22, if the rotor RPM drops below 70 percent, it is said to be unrecoverable; you will probably crash and die. On this particular flight, the student froze up on the controls and the RPM quickly dropped below 70 percent. I was telling him to lower the collective but he just put it about halfway down and stopped. I tried to push my collective down but he had a death grip on his, preventing me from moving it. He was frightened to the point that he could not move. I saw 65 percent on the RPM gauge, but no matter how hard I pushed, I could not get the collective down. As a last-ditch effort, I punched him hard on the shoulder and yelled at him to let go of the controls. This got his attention and I was able to restore control to the helicopter—only feet from hitting the ground.

There were many other instances like this one during the three years that I instructed in R22 helicopters. One time, I almost got killed by an R22 and I was not even in the helicopter! I had a student whom I "thought" was ready to solo. My usual technique on the first solo of a student was to fly around the airport traffic pattern with him or her for a few landings. When the student was comfortable I would get out of the helicopter at the end of the runway and instruct the student to make three landings alone.

On this particular day, the student lifted the helicopter into a somewhat shaky hover, and instead of taking off, he turned the helicopter to face me. Now, I was about fifty feet away, but for some reason he started hovering toward me. I began backing up, and he kept coming closer and closer, to the point that the rotor blades were almost over my head. I turned and started running to one side but he turned the helicopter and began following me. I began waving my arms, motioning for him to land the helicopter. I guess he finally got the message and turned the helicopter back to the runway to land.

The problem with this was that, when he turned the helicopter around, he was so close to me that the tail rotor swung around and I had to dive to the ground to keep it from hitting me. When he finally landed, I walked over and got in the helicopter and asked him, "What in the world are you doing?" He told me that he got frightened being in the helicopter alone and somehow in his mind, he decided that he wanted me back inside, so he started hovering the helicopter over to me. I've witnessed this other times in my career—when people are frightened, they sometimes do crazy things.

My most interesting experience flying an R22 was on my very first cross-country flight. I had bought the helicopter in California and was ferrying it back to Tennessee. At that time, I had a lot of airplane experience but was not yet rated to fly helicopters. I hired an instructor to fly with me back to Tennessee, giving me instruction along the way. It was a great trip, flying low level across the country. I even saw a large herd of wild horses and several ghost towns.

The R22 had a very limited fuel capacity, so we had to stop for fuel about every two hours. Most of the time, we followed the interstate highway because the helicopter had no navigation instruments except for a magnetic compass. Between El Paso and Pecos, the interstate highway dipped down to the south. This added a lot of miles, so we decided to take a shortcut across the desert.

Unfortunately, there were some very strong headwinds, which we were unaware of until it was too late. It was a clear day with great visibility and I could see Pecos on the horizon, but it was still some forty miles away when the low fuel warning light illuminated. In an R22 helicopter, when the low fuel warning light comes on, you only have enough fuel for about four or five minutes of flying. We were only flying at five hundred feet, so I looked down, and luckily, I found a good landing spot. We were on the ground in a couple of minutes. I shut down the helicopter and got out, already wishing that we had brought along some water. We were in the Texas desert in the middle of August and it was 110 degrees. We looked at the map and decided that the best course of action was to walk to the highway, get a ride into town, and hire someone with a truck to bring us back with some fuel. Just a couple of five-gallon cans of aviation fuel would get us to the Pecos airport. Looking at the map, we thought the highway was no more than seven miles away. Boy, were we wrong!

We walked and walked through the hot desert sun. There were only a few thorny bushes along the way, which offered no shade. After a couple of hours, we came across a watering trough that some ranchers must have placed there for their cattle. It did not look like the healthiest place to drink, but we were desperate and water is water when you are thirsty.

After another mile of walking, we came across this huge ravine that was probably thirty yards wide and maybe fifty feet deep. There was no way to get around it so we slid down the bank to the bottom, into what appeared to be a dry river bed. Directly across from us was a very steep climb up the other bank, so we decided to walk down the ravine to find a better place to climb out.

By this time we were very hot, very tired, and wanted to conserve our energy as much as possible. As we rounded a bend, about forty feet in front of us, we encountered the largest longhorn steer that I have ever seen. Its horns had to be six feet across. I think it was just as surprised to see us as we were to see it. It stood there for a second and then began dragging its front feet back and forth, snorting, and shaking its head. I looked to my left and to my right. The banks of this gully were very steep and made of soft sand. I did not think we could climb it. I knew if we turned and ran that the steer could easily run us down, especially in the sorry shape we were in.

My grandfather had owned cattle when I was a boy, and they often got out of the pasture. Many times, I had helped him round them back up. I knew from experience that if you ran from a bull, it would chase you. The flight instructor standing beside me must have thought I was crazy when I picked up a handful of sand and started running at the steer. When I got about ten feet away, I threw the sand at it while waving my arms and yelling. The steer immediately turned around and ran away.

The instructor walked up and looked at me kind of strangely. I just told him that I was too tired to run and too tired to climb up out of this gully, so the only thing left was to fight the steer. Of course, I knew all along that the steer would run. I found out later that longhorn cattle are quite different than the Black Angus cows my grandfather had. Longhorns are often mean and have been known to chase people down and kill them. I'm glad I didn't know that at the time.

We climbed out of the gully at the first opportunity, and by then it was getting dark. After another hour of walking, it was so dark that we were stumbling and falling about every ten steps. We did not want to sit down, even to rest, because we knew there were tarantulas, scorpions, and rattlesnakes in the desert. To make matters worse, coyotes started howling around us as though they were circling us.

Finally, we saw a light up ahead. It looked as if it was very close but turned out to be at least a mile away. When we finally got there, we saw that it was a porch light on a small house. There was an old pickup truck parked in front. We knocked on the door, and after some time a man answered. He looked frightened and began looking around, wondering how we had gotten there. We tried to explain that we had walked across the desert, but apparently he could not speak English.

I motioned with my hand for something to drink and this he understood. He walked back into the house and returned with a small plastic cup and handed it to me. He pointed to a barrel on the front porch. I opened up the lid and saw that the barrel was filled with water. This house was so far out in the desert that it had no running water, so they had to collect rainwater to drink. It didn't matter to me where it came from, and I drank several glasses. It was the best-tasting water I ever remember drinking.

By then, his whole family had come out onto the front porch. He had a wife and about six children, none of whom could speak a word of English. I motioned to the truck to try to get him to drive us into town, but he acted like he did not understand. I pulled out a $20 bill and again pointed to the truck. This time, he nodded his head up and down. You've got to love money—it's the universal language. We got in the truck along with him, his wife, and two of his kids. I guess he did not want to drive back home alone. I hardly blame him. We were so far out in the desert it took us forty-five minutes in the truck to reach a paved road.

He took us to the house of a friend who could speak English. This man was very nice and took us to a hotel. By then it was almost midnight, and we were very hungry and very tired. Naturally, the restaurant was closed, and the only room available at the hotel turned out to be the honeymoon suite. It had a heart-shaped bed with mirrors all over the walls and ceiling. I guess I could have considered this to be the final straw to end this exasperating day, already filled with a chain of near-disastrous events. However, I was too exhausted to contemplate the meaning or appreciate the humor. I grabbed some cover and a pillow and headed for the couch. I was asleep in two minutes.

The next day, we bought two five-gallon gas cans and went to the airport and filled them with aviation fuel. We rented a truck and a driver who was familiar with the area and set out to find the helicopter. Even though we thought we knew exactly where it was, it took us four hours to find it. We estimated that we had walked fifteen miles. The driver told us we were lucky that we did not spend the night in desert. He said the biggest rattlesnakes in the country were right in this location. We refueled the helicopter, paid off the driver, and then continued on with our trip to Tennessee.

So yes, I had been lucky to survive my R22 experiences, but some of the other pilots that I flew with were not so lucky. A student crashed the very first helicopter that I owned when he lost control during a hover. The helicopter was a complete loss, even though he never got more than two feet off the ground. Luckily, he was uninjured. I later learned that he was probably high on cocaine.

The fourth helicopter that I owned, I sold to one of my students. He began teaching a friend of his to fly, to save money, rather than hiring a certified flight instructor. While he was teaching an autorotation, he lost control and killed himself and the student.

One morning, I was awakened by the phone ringing. It was the police department advising me that one of my helicopters had been in a crash near Memphis, Tennessee. I drove out to the airport, and sure enough, my helicopter was missing. This turned out to be a very bizarre story.

I had been teaching this twenty-year-old woman for a couple of months. She would come every Saturday morning and pay me a with a hundred-dollar bill to take a lesson. She was a very quiet person and probably only weighed about ninety-five pounds soaking wet wearing combat boots. She was beginning to pick up the flying fairly well, but she still needed several more lessons before she was ready to solo.

I guess she thought she was ready to solo, though, because early one morning she stole my helicopter! Turns out, she had a boyfriend in prison in Memphis. Her intention all along, in learning to fly, was to break him out of prison. I did not find this out until later. All I knew was that someone had stolen my helicopter and crashed it in a field in Arkansas, just across the river from Memphis. A police officer met me at the airport and we drove down to the crash site.

When I first spotted the helicopter in the distance, it appeared to have only minor damage, but when I pulled up beside it I could tell it was a total wreck. She had somehow managed to land on the skids, but it was a hard landing and the skids broke. The engine was buried about a foot in the soft dirt of a plowed field, and the rotor blades were damaged.

After I verified with the policeman that it was my helicopter, he told me the full story. My student had stolen my helicopter with the intent of breaking her boyfriend out of prison. However, en route to the prison, the helicopter had run out of gas. I thought back to the night before. It just so happened that I had flown a very late flight and was too tired to refuel the helicopter, which I normally do, before putting it in the hangar. She just happened to have picked the one time that the helicopter was not full of fuel.

When the helicopter had run out of fuel, she had begun an autorotation, just as I had taught her. But, unfortunately, it was still twilight, and she did not see an electric power line running across the field that she had chosen to land in. She did see it at the last minute and had to make an abrupt maneuver to avoid it. This messed up her autorotation, but she still managed to land on the skids, just too hard.

The impact had hurt her back, but she still had managed to walk to a nearby farmhouse. She asked the farmer for a ride to a nearby gas station on the interstate highway. She told him that she would call a friend to come get her. On the way to the gas station, the farmer said, she began to double over and she started to cry because her back was hurting so much. He took her straight to the emergency room and then called the police.

When the police searched the helicopter, they found a map of the prison, along with fake IDs for one of the prisoners. They put two and two together and figured out what she was up to. I still cannot believe this little tiny girl, who had never flown a solo flight in the helicopter, would attempt to fly into a prison yard over a hundred miles away and break out a prisoner.

The policeman wanted me to press charges, but I insisted on talking to her first. Later that day, I called her hospital room. She was unable to talk, but I spoke to her dad. She had a broken back but would fully recover.

My helicopter insurance deductible was $5000. I told her dad that, even though I was upset, I would not press charges for her stealing my helicopter if he would pay me the $5000 deductible. I would tell the police that she was just an overzealous student, that she had permission to fly any time she wanted. He readily agreed and sent me a certified check the next day. Just after I had cashed the check, she was charged with attempting a prison break. I felt bad about keeping the money, but after all, she did crash my helicopter.

About eighteen months later, I was subpoenaed to her trial. The night before the trial, the boyfriend was shot and killed trying to escape prison again. This time, he had talked another young girl into smuggling a pistol into his jail cell. I guess this guy had a way with women.

So that made three out of the seven R22s that I had owned that had crashed. Maybe the guy at customs who hired me was right. Maybe I am good—or very, very lucky.

Now, over twenty years later, the Robinson R22 helicopter is the best-selling helicopter in the world. Once the flight instructing community learned how to manage its unusual flight characteristics, it turned out to be a great and safe helicopter for training. But back in the R22's early days, when I got hired by customs for having survived eighteen hundred hours of flying this helicopter, it was an astounding feat—at least in the mind of the person who hired me. And that's all that really mattered to me.

CHAPTER THREE

It took nine months for the government to process the paperwork so that I could begin work for the United States Customs Service. Let me clear up some confusion before we proceed: There is no longer a federal agency known as the United States Customs Service. When the Department of Homeland Security was created in 2003, following the 9/11 attacks, 22 federal agencies were consolidated into one. After more than two hundred years of proud service, the US Customs Service became known as US Customs and Border Protection (CBP). Thus, I began my federal career in 1986 with US Customs, and later ended up in CBP within the Department of Homeland Security. That's only important because, for the first eighteen years of my career, I'll refer to customs, and for the last five years, I'll refer to CBP or Homeland Security. Same thing, different uniform.

It took nine months to process my paperwork because I was required to obtain a secret security clearance to become a federal law enforcement officer. This requires a thorough background investigation. An investigator interviews the applicant's neighbors, coworkers, friends, and relatives. The investigators check whether you have any kind of criminal record as well. A DUI or even a lot of speeding tickets can disqualify an applicant. They also check your financial records. The background check is done when an agent is hired and again every five years during his or her career.

Security clearances are taken very seriously by our government. Even so, it does not normally take nine months to do a background check. It turned out that the agent in charge of my background check lost the paperwork for several months, and it wasn't until the Air Branch called him to find out my status that he remembered that he was even working on my case. So much for the efficiency of the federal government. But it did not deter me; I was still excited about this job.

Maybe the adventure this job promised interested me because of where I was raised. I grew up in McNairy County, Tennessee—the place where legendary Sherriff Buford Pusser was "Walking Tall" as the county sheriff while I was in high school. I knew him personally, and all the drama in my small home town during my impressionable teen years may have influenced my adventuresome spirit.

I did not know just what to expect when I walked into the New Orleans Air Branch, located at the Belle Chasse Navy Base. The navy base was located on the banks of the Mississippi River just about seven miles—as the crow flies—from downtown New Orleans. It was pretty much in the swamps. It was a combined military base and had aircraft squadrons from not only the navy, but also the marines, the air force, coast guard, and of course US Customs. For a pilot, it was an exciting place to work.

When I first arrived at the New Orleans Air Branch, it had one Citation jet, one Blackhawk helicopter, one Huey helicopter, two Piper Navajos, and one Cessna 210 aircraft. They had a total of seven pilots, two of whom were away in training. They were in desperate need of pilots. I was told that no pilots had been hired for quite some time, but there were plans to hire many more pilots in the near future. I guess that was right, because within one year the branch had more than twenty pilots; two years later, we had more than thirty. When the branch started hiring in large numbers, thousands of pilots applied for the jobs and the application procedure became very competitive and complex.

I was lucky to get in before all this happened; I don't think I would have had the patience to endure the new application process. Currently it is a yearlong process that requires multiple interviews and flight checks. There are probably a thousand applicants for every one pilot that CBP hires. It's all about timing and I was just lucky that my timing was great.

I was glad to see that the branch had Navajo airplanes because I already had over a thousand hours of flight time in that type of airplane. Before opening my helicopter flight school, I had flown charter for a company in Tennessee. I'd flown passengers all over the United States and had also made countless flights carrying car parts from Tennessee to all the big automobile manufacturing plants in the North. Some of these parts were cushions used in car seats. They were lightweight but bulky, and we would often pack the airplane with so many that I was trapped inside the cockpit. I would get in the cockpit and then they would finish packing and shut the door. I actually had a hatchet in the cockpit to cut my way out if I had to make an emergency landing and there was no one to open the door and remove some of the cushions. Believe it or not, this was FAA approved. Anyway, I was glad to see at least one aircraft that I was familiar with.

By the afternoon of the first day, I was already on my first flight, in a Navajo. We flew south to where the mouth of the Mississippi River meets the Gulf of Mexico. Then we flew very low along the Louisiana coastline looking for bales of marijuana that had washed ashore. There had been an airdrop a few days earlier and people were reporting bales of marijuana floating ashore. We did not spot any marijuana, so we climbed up to a higher altitude and flew out into the Gulf of Mexico. It was my first time flying in this area, and I could not believe how many oil rigs were there. Today there are thousands of oil rigs in the Gulf of Mexico. Coming back to the airport at the end of the flight, we made a loop around the city of New Orleans before we landed. This ended my first flight with US Customs. The Gulf of Mexico and the swamps of southern Louisiana was a different environment from what I was familiar with. I ended up patrolling this area, along with the coastline from Florida to Texas, for eighteen years with the New Orleans Air Branch.

On my second day with customs, I flew the Huey helicopter. It was an old army hand-me-down and had seen action in Vietnam as a gunship. It was an easy and fun helicopter to fly. Back in those days, the customs aviation program was not as structured as it is today. No one wore uniforms, and most pilots wore blue jeans, a T-shirt, and tennis shoes. It was not until years later that we began wearing flight suits.

In flying the aircraft, we had the same casual attitude. On my first flight in the Huey, I looked around for a checklist. A checklist is kind of a go-by that is used in all aircraft to make sure that critical procedures are not forgotten. The Huey had no checklist—not even a flight manual. The instructor pilot whom I was flying with told me that all the helicopter pilots before me had flown Hueys in the military and therefore had memorized all the checklist procedures. That was fine for them, but I had never even been inside a Huey before.

After three flights and a total of three and a half hours of flight time, I was signed off as a pilot in command of the Huey. After I made PIC I went to one of the pilots whom I had befriended and asked him to help me write down the starting procedure. I was a pilot in command, properly signed off to fly people and missions, and I did not even know how to start the helicopter! By the time I retired, a new pilot would have to go through several schools and a detailed flight syllabus at the branch, all of which could take up to a year, before he would be allowed to fly as PIC in any aircraft. It is amazing that I survived those early years.

A few days later, I got my first flight in the Blackhawk. This was a large state-of-the-art military helicopter, and I was very excited to get to fly it. Actually, my flight was against regulations; I was not supposed to fly it. Because of the size of this helicopter, it requires two pilots. Both pilots must have attended a military flight school, because these helicopters were actually on loan from the army. However, a law enforcement emergency arose that day, and I was one of only two helicopter pilots available.

We had gotten information that a load of cattle had been brought up from Mexico with cocaine hidden inside them. The cattle were supposedly at a farm in central Louisiana. Special Agents requested that we do a flyover to verify that the cattle were there, so they could get a warrant and search the farm. We had to leave immediately, before the cattle were slaughtered and the cocaine was removed from the farm. Lucky for me, I was again in the right place at the right time.

We had no time for me to get a brief on operating this helicopter. I did not even know how to put on the somewhat complex seatbelt. Within minutes we were lifting off the ground, and before we were ten feet in the air, my door popped open. It turned out that closing and locking the door was something else I did not know how to do.

Once we leveled off at altitude, the other pilot gave me the controls. I had always heard that the bigger the aircraft is, the easier it is to fly. I have found this statement to be true throughout my career. The Blackhawk had a stability augmentation system, a kind of hydraulic assist of the flight controls. This made the helicopter very easy to fly in level flight. You could actually let go of the cyclic for short periods of time and the helicopter would remain straight and level. If you let go of a cyclic in an R22, for even a few seconds, the helicopter would be upside down.

When we reached the farm, we found all the cattle dead. There was a big pile of charred flesh thrown into in a large hole that someone had dug out with a backhoe. The cattle had obviously been doused with gas and burned. However, there were enough remains to clearly see what was once about thirty head of cattle. I'm sure the smugglers had intended to bury the remains, but we had gotten there in time, so we were able to open an investigation. I heard later that arrests were made.

I had spent only two weeks at the New Orleans Air Branch when I was scheduled for a sixteen-week course at the Federal Law Enforcement Training Center (FLETC) in Glynco, Georgia. Almost all federal agencies were sending people there to be trained as federal law enforcement officers of one kind or another. I rented a condo on the beach at St. Simons Island and began training. I could have stayed for free at the academy, but I preferred to live on the beach on my own dime. It turned out to be one of my better decisions. The academy was very intense, and it was nice to be able to get away on nights and weekends.

The academy was pretty much what you would expect of a police academy on steroids. There were classes on law, search and seizures, customs laws, etc. We also had classes on firearms, and everyone had to qualify with several different weapons. There were classes on self-defense and lots of physical training. At times, I thought that I was back in the army. We also had classes on fingerprinting and how to work crime scenes.

I found most of the training to be very interesting, but I was glad when it was over. Even though I was now a gun-carrying federal law enforcement officer, I was still a pilot at heart and could not wait to get back into the cockpit. At the graduation ceremony, they presented us with our gold badges and duty pistols. To illustrate how long ago that was, my duty pistol was a revolver. In 1987, that was considered by customs to be the best weapon an officer could have. Of course, within a few years, all federal agencies and almost all state and local law enforcement officers were using semi-automatic pistols. The accuracy, rate of fire, and fast reloading capability of semi-automatics make them far superior to revolvers.

By the time I returned to the New Orleans Air Branch, we had gotten a new airplane. It was a Cheyenne III turboprop. Like the Citation, it was equipped with air-to-air radar and an infrared camera. We called it the CHET, for Customs High Endurance Tracker. This aircraft could stay airborne for up to six hours, so it had an incredible range. This was another lucky break for me; I had over a thousand hours flying Cheyennes before coming to customs.

I was flying charter services for a man in Tennessee who made millions in gold when it shot up to over $800 an ounce in the early 1980s. At the time, I was flying him back and forth to Washington, D.C. He was attempting to get approval to build a refinery that would convert soybeans into a product that could be used in gasoline. He decided that he needed a faster airplane, so I sold him an $870,000 Cheyenne II. The dealer paid me $9000 in commission. That was a very good day. I flew it for a couple of years, until we had to sell it after the man died mysteriously of a gunshot wound. Some believe he was murdered. I never did find out exactly what happened.

Within months of returning to the branch, I was flying the CHET and four other aircraft. Our air branch's area of responsibility (AOR) was the coastline from Florida to Texas, the Gulf of Mexico, and about six states. Of course, being a federal agency we had jurisdiction throughout the United States. There were also six other Customs Air Branches across the southern United States and we would help each other whenever there was a major operation.

Soon, I was scheduled to help the Houston Air Branch on an operation. There was considerable air smuggling going on in their AOR. Airplanes loaded with dope would fly up from Mexico and Central America and try to enter the United States over remote sections of the Texas coastline. With the help of several additional aircraft from other air branches, Houston planned a two-week operation to patrol the coastline, around the clock. I was assigned as a pilot on the CHET.

Late one night, while on patrol a hundred miles or so out in the Gulf of Mexico, the CHET's radar picked up a target. We intercepted the target and found it to be a large four-engine, propeller-driven airplane.

Smugglers normally use smaller type airplanes but you never know, this could be the mother lode. It was very dark, and we had to pull up close behind the aircraft in order to get the number on the tail, in hopes of identifying the owner. As we covertly sneaked up to the airplane we could see people through the passenger windows. It turned out to be a scheduled Mexican airliner! We turned away from the target as quickly as possible in hopes that no one had seen us.

On another night during this operation, a ground radar controller picked up a target crossing the coastline and landing at a small airport just south of Houston. This was about 2:00 in the morning, and the plane fit the profile of the targets we were looking for. I was over thirty minutes away in the CHET, but I headed there at top speed. A Blackhawk scrambled out of Houston and beat me to the airport. By the time I arrived overhead with the CHET, the Blackhawk was hovering around the airport searching with its powerful five million candlepower searchlight.

We began circling the airport, using the infrared camera to try and locate any aircraft whose engines were still hot. Suddenly we got a call from the Blackhawk saying that they needed to return to base. This seemed a little unusual, seeing as we were right in the middle of searching for a suspect airplane, but the call sounded urgent. They requested that we escort them back to the air branch.

After we had both landed I walked over to the helicopter to see what the problem was. Before I arrived at the helicopter, I could see the problem. The Blackhawk helicopter is on wheels instead of skids. The right wheel hung at an odd angle. What had happened to them has almost happened to me on numerous occasions. When you're hovering very low and looking at the ground with the searchlight, which can move in any direction, it is very easy to get disoriented. On this occasion, the pilot had hit the ground going sideways, and he'd bent the landing gear strut. It ended up costing over $100,000 to repair.

One morning, I was eating breakfast with another pilot from New Orleans at the hotel where we were staying in Houston. Houston is the national corporate headquarters of Continental Airlines and it just so happened that they were interviewing pilots at that same hotel. The pilot with whom I was eating breakfast recognized one of the Continental recruiters as an old Army buddy. The recruiter ate breakfast with us, and by the time we had finished, he had offered both of us jobs as airline pilots. I had always thought I wanted to be an airline pilot, but that was before the customs job. I could already tell that this job was going to be much more exciting than being an airline pilot could ever be.

I turned the job down but the other pilot didn't. Within months, he was flying the "heavy metal." Now, more than two decades later, I'm certainly glad I made that decision. He was furloughed several times during his career and has no retirement pension. The number one thing that I had as a government pilot was job security. There was always a steady paycheck and now a great pension. I would have other opportunities during my career to fly for the airlines, but I was having too much fun with customs.

The stint in Houston ended my first operation with customs. Over the next twenty-three years, I would be involved in operations throughout the United States and a dozen other countries.

CHAPTER FOUR

One of the things I liked most about working for customs was the lack of routine. You never knew from one day to the next what aircraft you would be flying or what the mission would be. For that matter, you never knew what city you would end up in at the end of the day, or even what country.

One night, I was assigned to fly the Citation jet. We had some intelligence that a shrimp boat was going to attempt to offload a large load of marijuana in one of the bayous of southern Louisiana. My job was to patrol along the coastline and try and locate this boat. We had the name and color of the boat, but finding it from the air was quite a challenge, especially at night. You cannot see colors on an infrared camera. It was always quite a joke when we would get sent out to find a shrimp boat in the Gulf of Mexico. Depending on what time of the year it was, there could be anywhere from ten to a thousand shrimp boats, and they all looked the same.

But the intel we had for this particular case was exceptional, and we found the boat entering a bayou just as predicted. I circled overhead for hours, lights out, as the boat worked its way through the swamps. These swamps were the exact same area that the pirate Jean Lafitte had used to evade the entire US Navy nearly two hundred years before. I'm quite sure that the smugglers on the boat were very confident that no one could find them so deep in these swamps.

While I was circling, I was talking to agents on the ground who were assembling a small army of law enforcement personnel to arrest the smugglers once they stopped. A load this large would also have a large number of people to help offload it quickly. There could be as many as ten or fifteen guys, probably armed, deep in the swamps. Whenever we confronted a situation like this, we tried to have overwhelming numbers of our own guys to overcome the target's guys.

I was getting low on fuel, but if I took my eyes off the boat to refuel we might never have been able to find it again. To my surprise, the boat was getting closer and closer to the Belle Chasse Navy Base. Unbelievably, the boat actually stopped to offload in a small canal just five miles from my office. Since I was, in effect, circling right over the airport I could almost glide in for landing if I ran out of fuel. This allowed me to fly until I had the minimum amount of fuel reserves I needed to land. I ended up flying 5.2 hours in the Citation, which was a record amount of flight time on one tank of fuel.

The shrimp boat finally pulled over to the bank and tied up. Through the infrared camera, I could see several pickup trucks approach the boat. I knew the offload was about to begin. In minutes, the marijuana would be unloaded, and the trucks would scatter in all directions. It was important to direct the ground forces in quickly. They were positioned in Belle Chasse, no more than five miles away. So when I called, it was only a minute before I could see them coming, in a long line of about ten police vehicles, all with blue lights on.

We guided them down a gravel road parallel to the canal where the shrimp boat was offloading. The problem was that the smugglers had made a dirt road through a cow pasture to reach the boat. This dirt road was impossible to see at night from the air, especially because they had put a fence across it and cattle were running around everywhere. We tried to direct the police vehicles the best we could, but they could not find a way to reach the boat. Finally, one of the larger trucks rammed the fence, breaking it down but also destroying the front of the truck. Now all the vehicles could get to the boat—but the bad guys now saw them coming.

They began to run in every direction. From the air it looked pretty comical, almost like a bunch of Keystone Kops. There were probably thirty law enforcement officers and ten bad guys and a hundred cows. It was very dark, so we could only see with the infrared camera. It was impossible to tell good guys from bad guys. Finally, we radioed to the ground for all the officers to stand in a group, which they did. Then we could direct them to where the bad guys were hiding.

We ended up arresting ten smugglers, seizing the boat, and seizing over 38,000 pounds of marijuana. It was a good night's work, and I still cannot believe that it all happened less than five miles from my office.

We later used this boat in undercover operations. Customs agents would pretend to be shrimpers who were willing to smuggle drugs. One night, while one of my colleagues was patrolling in the Citation far out in the Gulf of Mexico, he overheard a mayday call over the radio. It turned out to be customs agents on an undercover operation in this boat. They were in a gun battle off the coast of Colombia. We coordinated some help from a nearby navy vessel and the agents managed to return safely. They speculated there were casualties to the bad guys.

Less than a year later, I was involved in the seizure of another shrimp boat loaded with marijuana. Again, this one was in the swamps and bayous of southern Louisiana. We had gotten information from an informant that a large load of marijuana was to be offloaded in a remote bayou south of Lake Charles, Louisiana.

Since there was the possibility of a large group of bad guys, we decided to take two helicopters. I was flying the Huey helicopter and flew formation from New Orleans to Lake Charles with the Blackhawk. Since the Huey was much slower than the Blackhawk, the Blackhawk had to fly slowly so that I could keep up. This slow flight by the Blackhawk would create a comical chain of events later that night.

As normal, the offload of the shrimp boat was going to take place in the middle of the night. Why smugglers could not operate in the middle of the day is a mystery to me. They always wanted to do their business at the most inconvenient time for me. Not only was it 1:00 am, but it was a very cold night. It was so cold that while we were preparing the helicopters to take off, it was snowing. No one could remember having snow in southern Louisiana. I was lucky that the helicopter had a heater. The bad guys would have a cold miserable night running through the swamps.

We took off from Lake Charles just after midnight, and within seconds I knew I had a problem. I had almost no tail rotor control with my foot pedals. I did not know if the sub-freezing temperatures had something to do with this, but I knew I had a hydraulic problem.

I managed to come back and land the helicopter, but it was one of the most difficult landings I had ever done. With no hydraulics, it takes a great deal of pressure on the controls to maintain control of the helicopter.

Only minutes after landing and consulting with a mechanic I found the problem was all my fault. On the previous landing I had failed to drain the hydraulics from one tank to another. Since this Huey was an old 1960 model, the pilot had to manually drain a hydraulic line after each flight. This is always a messy operation where you often ended up with hydraulic fluid all over your hands. It had been so cold when I landed that I didn't want to mess with this step.

What could it hurt to skip this just one time?

Thirty minutes later, the helicopter was fixed and I was back in the air heading for the shrimp boat. The Blackhawk was already on the scene. The boat had been spotted coming up a bayou as well as several offload vehicles. The offload vehicles consisted of two pickup trucks and a large U-Haul rental truck. There were ten or more people around the trucks and an unknown number of people on the boat. We had four officers in each helicopter and maybe another fifty on the ground. We had the place surrounded as much as possible without being seen.

When they began unloading the boat, we decided to make our move. I swooped low over the boat and turned on my spotlight. The Blackhawk hovered over the trucks and turned on its spotlight. When the cold dark swamp turned to daylight the bad guys scattered like cockroaches. They ran in every direction.

The driver of the U-Haul truck took off at full speed down a dirt road. Police officers on the ground had set up a roadblock about a half-mile down this road. The U-Haul truck driver obviously did not want to give up and decided to ram the roadblock in hopes of escaping. Officers standing behind the cars opened fire with rifles. The driver was shot in the shoulder and veered off the road and hit a tree.

Because we were in such a remote area, the Blackhawk was called in to medevac the driver to the hospital. It picked up the wounded driver and headed to the nearest hospital, which was forty miles away. About halfway to the hospital, the pilots suddenly realized they were flying at the same slow speed at which they had flown over from New Orleans. In all the excitement, they were just using the same power settings that they had just used on the previous three-hour flight from New Orleans. They sped up and got the wounded man to the hospital still alive. The agents in the back of the helicopter were upset that the smuggler had bled all over their equipment.

Meanwhile, I was hovering over the scene trying to direct law enforcement officers to the bad guys hiding in the swamps. I was overhead just as a customs boat loaded with agents arrived at the shrimp boat. The agents on board the customs boat did not realize that local police officers had already boarded the boat. As they pulled up, they saw one man coming out of the boat carrying a long gun. One agent took aim and was about to pull the trigger when he noticed a blue arm band on the man, who was a local officer. That little piece of cloth saved the officer's life.

This operation involved not only federal but also state and local law enforcement personnel. Because there were so many different organizations involved, in order to help tell the good guys from the bad guys all the officers were issued an arm band. Had the officer not been wearing the armband, the agent surely would have shot him.

After several hours, we had rounded up all the bad guys we could find. We decided we would come back at daybreak, when we could see better, to find the last three smugglers who were still hiding in the swamps. I flew back to my hotel in Lake Charles and got about three hours of sleep before it was time to return.

Again, I took off in the Huey along with the Blackhawk. We divided up the area and began what we assumed would be a long day of searching. Within minutes, though, the three remaining smugglers ran out of the swamps with their hands up. After we picked them up, they said that they had nearly frozen to death in the swamp during the night. As soon as they saw our helicopters, they were more than ready to give up. We ended up making a dozen arrests, seizing another boat and almost 40,000 pounds of marijuana.

Within my first year of working for customs, I had been in on two large seizures involving boats. I was anxious to get in on an airplane chase. After all, aircraft smuggling was one of the main reasons that US Customs had an air interdiction program. From about 1984 to 1987, aircraft were coming across our southern borders in large numbers, smuggling drugs. The smuggling was totally out of control, and since the US Customs Service had the job of protecting our borders, it was the logical agency to use to prevent the air smuggling. A huge amount of money from Congress was given to customs to build the small aviation department into the world's largest law enforcement air force. During my first two years with the customs air program, the number of aircraft and agents increased five-fold.

I remember a funny story that illustrates just how bad the smuggling was. A county sheriff, located in southern Florida, was giving a speech during a campaign rally in a large parking lot. He was trying to convince the audience that he would stop smuggling in his county. During the speech, an airplane was seen in the background, air dropping a load of drugs. Cameras actually caught the event on live TV. I never heard if the sheriff was re-elected.

It didn't take much more than a year or two after US Customs built up its aviation program before air smuggling began to taper off drastically. We set up radar in unsuspected places. When we added our new Citation jets, with their air-to-air radar capabilities, the smuggling aircraft were like sitting ducks those first few months. It did not take long for the smugglers to realize that it was now a lot harder to smuggle drugs into the United States by air. I wanted to get involved in an airplane chase and seizure before they quit smuggling by aircraft altogether. I needn't have worried. I would get in plenty of aircraft chases. My first chase was not long after the Lake Charles incident.

I was assigned the Citation for the day and was just about to do a radar patrol when the scramble alarm sounded. That meant that my crew and I had eight minutes to get into the air. Once airborne, customs ground-based radar controllers would give us a vector to the target. This particular target was spotted on radar crossing into the United States from outside the ADIZ (Air Defense Identification Zone). This ADIZ is the line around the United States that separates foreign from domestic flights. This airplane appeared to have originated from Mexico and was skirting around the US coastline. It fit the profile of a smuggler perfectly.

I intercepted the suspect target just south of Grand Isle, Louisiana. I turned behind it covertly about three miles in trail. Slowly, I pulled my jet up close enough behind to read the airplane's tail number. My co-pilot radioed the number in to our dispatch office (called sector and located in south Florida) to verify that it was on a flight plan and to identify the registered owner. We also ran the aircraft and owner through our computer database to see if there was any prior history of smuggling.

We learned nothing derogatory about the plane or the owner, but it didn't matter. The plane had entered into the United States illegally so I backed off into a two mile trail position and set in to follow it to wherever it was going. Yet, this flight could still be legal. Its flight plan could have been lost by the FAA or the pilot could be lost or just stupid. I had seen it all numerous times already in my short customs career. But somehow, this plane seemed different. I got a strange feeling in my gut. I had heard about this phenomenon before. Law enforcement officers commonly got gut feelings that something was not right. I had always thought it was fiction. I don't think that now. It is real. But this was my first experience with the feeling and it was very strange indeed.

The plane started descending just outside Gulfport, Mississippi. We monitored the Gulfport control tower frequency, and sure enough, the plane radioed that it was landing there. We contacted the control tower on a separate and secure frequency and identified ourselves with our law enforcement call sign. We told the tower we planned on landing behind the airplane and executing an enforcement stop.

Nothing is ever simple. I had to plan the landing just the right distance behind the suspect airplane so that I could stop beside it as it turned off its engines. But not too close, or I might run into it before it turned off the runway. While I was computing all this out in my mind and spacing myself accordingly, a heavy rain shower started right over the airport. I was on final approach, perfectly spaced, when the rain hit just as the plane touched down. It was raining so hard that I lost visual contact with the ground. There was no way I could land behind the other plane now for fear the plane might stop on the runway and I would crash into it. I knew that, if I didn't get on the ground quickly, the pilot could be gone by the time we got there.

I noticed that the rain shower was intense but was small and I saw that another runway on the airport was in the clear. Getting the tower's permission I quickly switched over to the other runway. Now, this runway was in a different direction, so I was not set properly to land. I was way too high. I put the Citation into a slip, a maneuver where you cross-control the rudder and ailerons. The airplane falls out of the sky almost sideways when you do this. Actually, you are not supposed to slip a jet. Air cannot go into the engines correctly and you could have a flame-out. But I had to get down. There was no way I was going to let the pilot of my first airplane chase get away!

I got the jet down safely and pulled up behind the suspect plane just as it was shutting down its engine. We jumped out and greeted the pilot as he was getting out of the airplane. He was very surprised. This was the first time since we had intercepted him—over an hour earlier—that he knew we were anywhere around. That's the way it was supposed to be.

He acted nervous as we searched his luggage. For good reason—one bag was filled with marijuana. It was only a fifty-pound load but it was my first airplane chase that resulted in a seizure.

Just a few days later, I was assigned to fly the CHET up to Arkansas for maintenance. That was during the time that Jesse Jackson was running for president. While I was sitting in the lobby of the Little Rock Airport, waiting for my aircraft, he pulled up in an airplane. I watched Jackson get out of the small airplane and come inside, leaving his Secret Service protection agents standing beside the airplane. I guess he was in a hurry to use the restroom. And I guess the Secret Service thought it was safe to leave him unprotected. As he passed me in the lobby, he nodded. I looked around and it was only him and me. This was a time when customs pilots did not wear uniforms, so I was wearing blue jeans, a T-shirt, and an ankle holster holding a 38 caliber pistol. I could've been any nut off the street. So much for Secret Service protection!

About a month later, a film crew from the TV show *America's Most Wanted* showed up at the office. They were there to film an episode about a case we had done months earlier. Some of the other pilots had chased an airplane loaded with drugs all the way to Tennessee. The plane had landed in a remote Tennessee airport after a daring chase involving customs Citation jets and Blackhawk helicopters. Immediately on landing, the pilot of the drug plane had set it on fire and escaped. We tracked him down and arrested him a few days later and found out he had smuggled several prior loads. He had been wanted by the DEA for a long time. It was the capture of a famous fugitive, so *America's Most Wanted* requested that we reenact the airplane chase.

I was honored to be chosen to fly the Citation for the reenactment. We used one of our single engine airplanes to act as the smuggler. For over two hours, I flew intercept after intercept on this aircraft while the cameraman filmed from a third airplane. I just knew that with all this filming of my great piloting skills, I would no doubt become very famous. When the episode aired on TV, all my hours of flying was reduced to about fifteen seconds. You hear about fifteen minutes of fame—I only got fifteen seconds. Oh well, maybe another time.

CHAPTER FIVE

Due to the rapid growth in the number of customs pilots, there was no way that all of us could be trained locally. Customs decided to start a three-week air tactical training course in Marana, Arizona. This was a small government facility located on a large airstrip in the desert about sixty miles north of Tucson. The purpose of this training was to standardize our air tactics so that all the pilots from around the country were performing tactical maneuvers the same way. There were now a lot of national operations and it was common to fly with pilots from another air branch, so everyone needed to be on the same sheet of music.

I was asked to fly the Citation from New Orleans to Marana and give the new pilots going through this course an orientation flight, demonstrating proper tactics. Marana was in the area of the supposed lost Dutchman gold mine. This mine allegedly was shown by Indians to the first Spanish explorers of what would become the western United States. It was said that there was a large amount of gold just lying on the ground. The Indians would not allow the Spanish to pick up any of the gold and, for a variety of reasons, they never were able to return. People have been searching for this mine ever since.

So here I was with the freedom to fly over this remote area with an infrared camera that was capable, I hoped, of picking up any hot reflections of the gold lying on the ground. Well, I incorporated a thorough search of the desert into my tactics training. Unfortunately, no gold was found. It had been another one of my stupid ideas.

I did, however, find another treasure of sorts. On one of the weekends we were off work, I walked out into the desert to a place that a local resident had told me was where Geronimo had once camped. I did find some pieces of Indian pottery with paintings on it. It wasn't gold, but it was interesting.

One other thing that was interesting in Marana was the airplanes at this airport. Because of the low humidity and lack of rust, airlines stored their old or unused airplanes there. There were probably a hundred or more airliners parked all around the airport. There were several huge Boeing 747s parked there also. Some of them were undergoing some maintenance. It was rumored that the CIA used this airport to install cameras and other covert instrumentation aboard aircraft that resembled ordinary airliners.

It had only been a few months since the Chinese had shot down a US commercial airliner filled with passengers. They had accused the plane of spying on them. Of course, the United States denied any spying. The tail number of the 747 airliner that was shot down was recognized by one of our pilots. He swears that he saw that 747 in Marana only a week before the incident. Could our government use a commercial airliner as cover for a spy mission? I'll let you be the judge.

I was flying the Huey on a bayou patrol. In the back were several new hires we called Air Interdiction Officers (AIO). They were not pilots but usually had a great deal of police experience, either at the state or local level. They were taught to operate the radar and infrared camera equipment in the Citation and the CHET and were used as tactical team members on the helicopters. These AIOs played an important role in the law enforcement side of the customs aviation program. They were the experts in conducting investigations and teaching us pilots police tactics. They knew a lot about police work but almost nothing about flying.

The Huey had a large sliding door on the side and we would sometimes fly with it open. The new officers in the back decided to open this door in flight without informing me. The problem was that this door is only supposed to be opened while on the ground or while hovering to prevent aerodynamic forces from ripping it off the helicopter.

As we were flying along, one of the officers called me over the intercom and said he thought the door had come off. I quickly learned that they had tried to open it in flight and, sure enough, the wind blew it off the helicopter. Not good. Three bad things could have easily happened.

First, the door could have struck the tail, resulting in major damage and causing us to crash. Second, the door could have hit the tail rotor and we would have been in for an interesting landing, if we could have landed at all. Third, the door could have hit someone on the ground. Fortunately, we were flying over the swamps so the only things below us were snakes and alligators. It would have been okay with me to take out either.

Air smuggling into the United States began to drop off drastically due to our increased efficiency in interdicting the smugglers. For the first time, we had the proper amount of pilots and aircraft to do our job. The smugglers soon realized that things had changed and they could no longer safely smuggle by air into the United States. So they simply changed their tactics. They began to make air drops to boats waiting offshore.

There was some of this activity in the Gulf of Mexico, so I spent a lot of time doing radar patrols in the gulf. But most of the airdrops were happening in the Caribbean, in places such as the Bahamas, Puerto Rica, and Cuba. US Customs began to set up operations in these areas. During my career, I traveled to these places over a dozen times to work on operations. Normally a trip would last about thirty days. Most of the time I flew the Citation jet, but I did make several trips to Puerto Rico, where I flew the Blackhawk.

My first trip to the Caribbean was to Cuba. Castro was still in charge, and he was allowing drug smugglers to use his island, if they paid his price. Typically, a plane would fly up from Colombia and airdrop its drugs to a boat inside a twelve-mile ring around Cuba. Cuba claimed the waters out to twelve miles around it as part of its territorial boundaries. Due to international agreements between the United States and Cuba, this area was off limits to us.

Cuba was very protective of these waters and often launched Migs (fighter jets) to intercept us if we got too close. They would also interrogate us with surface-to-air missile radar systems to keep us out of this area. With the radar onboard our Citations, we had the capability of knowing if military radar was looking at us.

I assumed that they were just bluffing when they would 'light us up' with radar in order to scare us away. If they had shot us down, it would have created a major international incident, drawing a lot of unwanted attention to Cuba. Anyway, that's what I told myself.

I often flew just outside the twelve-mile boundary, ignoring all their radar threats. We would see drug planes entering this area and dropping their loads to boats below. We knew the Cubans were protecting the smuggling activities but there was nothing we could do about it. Sometimes I could see Cuban navy vessels within sight of the airdrop.

Years later, I interviewed a smuggler after he had been arrested and was in prison. He told me that he was allowed to fly directly over Cuba if he paid $100,000. This explained the many times I was chasing a suspect target south of Cuba and it would continue northbound over Cuba while I had to turn around at the twelve-mile boundary.

We based our Citations at Guantanamo Bay, a US military base in Cuba. This base was a huge thorn in the side to Cuba. They did not want us to be there, but the United States had a ninety-nine-year lease on this base that went back to the time of the Bay of Pigs and President Kennedy. The base is located on a small bay on the southeast side of Cuba. When flying an airplane in and out of this base we had to follow a very narrow air corridor. When landing at the airport to the east, we only had half a mile from the end of the runway until we'd enter Cuban airspace. So we had to make a very steep turn when turning to line up with the runway.

I thought this was a little tricky until I saw a C-5 Galaxy (the military's largest airplane) make this turn and land. After that I never complained. If that large aircraft could do it, so could I. Sometimes the Cubans would shoot lasers into the cockpits while we were making this turn to try the blind the pilots. They never succeeded in blinding anyone, but I did talk to one pilot who had suffered some minor effects.

Customs put two house trailers on the base, and the pilots stayed in them. The trailers were only about three miles from the border, which consisted of a heavily guarded barbed wire fence surrounded by land mines. One night, while I was sleeping, my trailer shook from a huge explosion. I woke up out of a deep sleep, not knowing exactly what had happened. Then another large explosion occurred and minutes later, still another. I thought at first maybe we were under attack, but the explosions stopped.

Since there was nothing I could do about it, I turned over and went back to sleep. The next morning I discovered that lightning had started a fire in the mine field, which was covered with dried grass. The grass fire was setting off the land mines. I was glad that I had not lost any sleep over this.

On our days off in Cuba we would go down to the ocean to snorkel and scuba dive. There were a lot of beautiful coral reefs in the area. I had the opportunity to scuba dive off several different islands throughout the Caribbean. What I remember most about diving in Cuba was that there were a great deal of spiny urchins. These small creatures—about the size of a tennis ball—were covered with long sharp needles. Divers had to be very careful to not step on one because, once embedded, these needles were extremely painful and difficult to remove.

On one trip, two pilots from the New Orleans Air Branch were out diving and went down to a depth of about a hundred and thirty feet. This is considered a very deep dive, given the equipment that we had. The rule of thumb I used was never to dive deeper than I could hold my breath long enough to reach the surface. What was most amazing about their dive is that one of the divers was on his very first scuba dive.

He had not received any training, he just did it. If anything had gone wrong, he would probably be dead. That's pretty much how all the pilots lived their lives. Nearly everyone had a Type A personality and did everything at one speed: full throttle.

I have to confess that one time I did dive below a hundred feet. There is this huge rift along the ocean floor that runs across the Caribbean. You can be diving along the ocean floor at about eighty feet and suddenly there's this huge cliff. It is like looking over the edge of the Grand Canyon, only with no bottom in sight. This is one of the most awesome sights I have ever seen.

The ocean floor instantly drops off to a depth of more than two miles. I was diving along the sandy ocean bottom, watching the fish, and suddenly I was hovering over the blue abyss. I felt this strange sensation of flying as I floated over this cliff. So, naturally, I had to swim down the cliff for a little way just to see what it was like. When the color of the coral growing along the sides began to fade out, I knew I was deep. The deeper you go, the less light there is, so color disappears and everything is black and white. I started back up and when I remembered to check my depth gauge I was still at 118 feet.

I also got to dive on an airplane and boat that were in the ocean off Nassau, in the Bahamas. The boat was used in a James Bond movie where a shark attacked him inside the boat. It was kind of strange being inside the boat where the shark was attacking Bond in the movie. I halfway expected to see a shark jump at me as I opened the door. I also dived on the airplane used in the James Bond movie *Thunderball*. Scuba diving is almost as much fun as flying. When I was in Aruba, I was able to take a trip in a submarine down to a hundred and fifty feet below the surface, which was also a lot of fun.

A few months after I returned from Cuba, another customs pilot who also enjoyed scuba diving came to me with a very interesting proposition. A friend of his had found a Spanish gold coin off the shore of Florida. He had taken this old gold coin to an expert and discovered that it was from a lost Spanish galleon that had sunk during a hurricane hundreds of years ago.

According to records, this ship was loaded with thousands of gold coins and had never been found. This coin was the first one that had ever been found. Apparently, the Spanish kept very good records and marked each coin to identify its lot and shipment.

Several of us customs pilots got together and rented a boat, brought some underwater metal detectors, and soon we were on a dive expedition to find this lost Spanish galleon. After several days of searching the area where the coin was found we had found nothing. We were all disappointed that we had not struck it rich.

A couple of years later, one of the pilots talked to an oceanography professor and was told that the ship, if it was there, was probably under thirty feet of sand. It would take a big salvage operation to conduct a thorough search. It was a much too big and costly project for us at the time, so we are saving that for another day.

By 1990, four years after I began working for customs, air smuggling began to really drop off. We were getting fewer and fewer targets to intercept. We now had over thirty pilots at the New Orleans Air Branch, which meant there were not enough aircraft for each pilot to fly every day.

We began doing criminal investigations in our five-state area of responsibility (AOR). We would visit all the small airports in our AOR, checking airplane registrations, and sometimes running the drug sniffing dogs on them.

Customs was handing out a lot of money to informants, hoping to gather information on possible smuggling operations. I spent a lot of time investigating suspicious activity throughout the states of Tennessee, Mississippi, Louisiana, and Arkansas. This led to the seizures of several aircraft that were being used for smuggling and several arrests.

While working in southern Arkansas, I checked an airport in Mena. Several old, military-type aircraft based there seemed out of place for a small airport in Arkansas. I did some research and discovered that this was allegedly the airport that had been used to smuggle arms into Nicaragua in the Contra arms scandal that led to the Congressional investigations.

This all happened while Bill Clinton was governor of Arkansas. Some news media asserted that Clinton knew all about what was going on in his state. I have no idea if any of these claims were true. What I knew for certain was that many people in Arkansas who supposedly had inside information had died under mysterious circumstances. These deaths were the subject of several television news shows and national newspaper investigative reports.

I personally investigated one such strange death. It just so happened that one of the key players in the Congressional Whitewater investigation was an old family friend. The family called me simply because they knew that I was a federal agent and someone they could trust. Murder investigations do not normally fall under the jurisdiction of US Customs Service, so I used the smuggling connection to conduct my investigation.

It wasn't long before I was convinced that my friend's death had been a murder. Customs management decided that this information should be turned over to the FBI. I called an FBI agent whom I had worked with in the past and presented my case. He said he would look into it and that he would pass on my information to the task force that was already conducting investigations into the other mysterious deaths in Arkansas.

I also investigated another smuggling operation that supposedly obtained cocaine from Mena, Arkansas. Basically, a mysterious group located in Arkansas had used biker gangs to distribute cocaine. There was little doubt that something big had once happened at this little airport in Arkansas, but it was all over by the time of my investigation. I could say more about this topic, but it is much too sensitive and could endanger people's lives. I can only give you the unclassified version of my investigation.

During this period, when the pilots were involved in investigations, we were also assisting state and local police departments a great deal. Since we had all the cool toys (airplanes and helicopters), they often called on us for help. We also assisted other federal agencies and were considered the informal federal air force. We soon realized that we needed a specialized team to assist in special missions and high risk warrants.

New Orleans was the first branch in the country to organize a SWAT (special weapons and tactics) Team. But law enforcement agencies all over the nation were adopting the new more politically correct term, Special Response Team (SRT). We called our team the "New Orleans Special Helicopter Interdiction Team" (NO SHIT). It kind of started as a joke, but soon caught on nationally.

We decided if we were going to start this team we were going to do it right. We brought in the top SRT trainers in the country from the energy department—the ones who protect the nuclear facilities across the country. We developed tough physical standards for pilots and enforcement officers who wished to join the team.

I made the team. It was hard training, but a lot of fun. We learned to execute high-risk search warrants and clear buildings, did sniper training, and did lots of shooting and self-defense practice. We also learned to rappel. I had to rappel forward and backward off a five-story building.

Our specialty was deploying the team by using the Blackhawk in an air interdiction. We would land behind a suspected drug smuggling airplane and have it surrounded before they knew we were even there.

The element of surprise made our job a lot safer because we never knew how many people were on a suspect airplane and how many weapons they had.

We also served high-risk warrants that were in remote areas where a helicopter was needed for access, as well as warrants in support of other federal, state, and local agencies. We had a large team with all the latest equipment. We even prepared to do a big job in Mexico, taking down an airliner-size airplane loaded with cocaine and protected by a large group of heavily armed mercenaries. That job was called off at the last minute due to political intervention.

Our NO SHIT team earned a national reputation. We were probably the best air interdiction SRT in the United States—possibly the best in the world. There was no one out there, outside of military special forces, that could do what we could do. Unfortunately, our reputation led to our downfall. In those early days of the air program, the Customs Air Branches worked independently.

The national command structure was mostly administrative. Each branch did things its own way. We were the only branch in the country with an SRT, and soon jealousy crept in. We were getting a lot of attention—some of it negative—at headquarters in Washington, D.C. They were asking, "Who authorized this team and why is it needed?"

Every few years, a different person was selected to be the national director of the Customs Air Program. We had a new director when the questioning of our team took place. He decided that it was not worth the trouble to fight for us, and we were told to disband.

CHAPTER SIX

After the NO SHIT days ended, I began to get heavily involved in undercover work. I was still flying patrols almost daily, but we didn't have a lot of real air targets so we were assisting the Customs Office of Investigations. They sometimes needed a pilot to go undercover, posing as a drug smuggler. Very few of the pilots wanted to do this type work because it was extremely dangerous.

My first undercover mission could have been straight out of a James Bond movie. In fact, it was. The Bond movie *Live and Let Die* depicted James Bond going to Jamaica to capture a notorious drug kingpin. That is exactly what I did!

US Customs special agents in San Diego arrested a big-time drug smuggler, and he decided to cooperate with us in hopes of getting less jail time. This particular smuggler had smuggled dozens of planeloads of marijuana and cocaine into the United States. His airplanes mostly flew out of Jamaica, so he worked with a smuggler there who was the number-one drug kingpin in the Caribbean.

Back in those days, we still called them kingpins. This guy was responsible for smuggling hundreds of thousands of pounds of marijuana and cocaine into the United States Somehow, of all the customs pilots in the United States, I was the one lucky enough, or crazy enough, to get this assignment.

My mission, if I decided to accept it, was to meet the Jamaica kingpin and get him to smuggle drugs into the United States, using me as the pilot. This would give us enough evidence to arrest him. Although we knew he was heavily involved in smuggling, we did not

44

yet have enough proof to arrest him. Also, since it was very difficult to extradite anyone from Jamaica, my mission was to get him to come into the United States. Maybe this was a "mission impossible."

We arranged for the smuggler we had recently arrested in San Diego, whom I will call Mr. X, to set up a meeting with the Jamaican kingpin where he would introduce me as his new pilot. We rented an expensive hotel suite in San Diego overlooking the marina. This was the kind of place the Jamaican, whom I will call Mr. Black, would expect the successful smuggler, Mr. X, to be staying. We got Mr. X out of jail and put him in the hotel room. Of course, we had several agents in the adjoining rooms.

I drove a car that was wired with a recording device to pick up Mr. Black and bring him back to the suite, where the three of us would plan out the smuggling operation. The hotel suite had audio and video recording devices so we could gather evidence of Mr. Black conspiring with me to smuggle illegal drugs into the United States.

The place where I was to meet Mr. Black was on a large sailboat in the San Diego Harbor. It was a historic ship that was used to sail from California to Australia in the 1890s. It was on display and anyone could pay a small fee and tour the ship. It had three tall masts and looked exactly like the ship used in the Tom Selleck movie, *Quigley Down Under.*

I don't know who was more nervous, him or me, when we first met. Somehow, he felt comfortable enough to get into the car with me and drive back to meet Mr. X. On the way to the hotel, he gave me a lecture on how to spend all the money I was going to be making smuggling for him. It was kind of a smuggler's advice on how not to get caught with large amounts of cash. I knew I would never have that problem, but it was an interesting conversation. I guess it's just such a burden to have too much cash.

We made it back to the suite, and Mr. X played his role perfectly. As soon as we arrived, he picked up the phone and ordered room service. He asked to speak directly to the chef and told him to forget the menu and prepare us a special meal. He named off a list of foods I could not even pronounce. He told the chef that money was no object. I could just imagine the expression on the face of the case agent in the next room as he watched all this on video and worried about paying the bill.

The meeting went well, and I was accepted as the new pilot. We agreed I would pick up a thousand pounds of marijuana and twenty gallons of hashish oil. Hashish oil was a potent liquid mixture of marijuana that Canadians were fond of. They would put a few drops on an ordinary cigarette and smoke it to get high. My pay was to be $300,000—and no, I was not tempted to really smuggle the drugs. I would turn down a lot more money than that on later undercover missions.

The airstrip that I intended to use in Jamaica was a dirt strip they had cut out of the jungle. It was decided that I would go down to Jamaica, via commercial airlines, to check this airstrip out in advance to make sure it was suitable. The load of drugs would be worth over $2 million, so we did not want there to be any problems with the airplane landing and taking off. We decided on a date, time, and place to meet again in Jamaica.

We no longer needed Mr. X, so he was taken back to prison. Before he left, he told me that I fit the role of a drug smuggling pilot perfectly. The pilots he had used in the past were all clean-cut corporate or airline pilots who would run a load or two on the side. I had thought that I looked a little too clean-cut, but I guess even smugglers expected their pilots to look professional. Go figure.

A few weeks later, I flew down on Delta Airlines to Montego Bay, Jamaica. My instructions were to check into the Holiday Inn and stand by. The kingpin's men would contact me when they determined things were safe. I stayed in my room for several hours after I checked in, waiting for them to contact me, but they never did. Finally, I left the room and went down to the beach to walk around. When I returned to my room, I discovered that my luggage had been searched. I knew this because I had set things up in a certain way so I would know if anyone had been in my room. I had removed all personal information from my possessions, so I was not worried about them discovering my true identity. I was using fake identification in the name of a high school friend, so it would be easy to remember.

Later, I would go to an undercover school at the Federal Law Enforcement Training Center and would learn that it is better to use your real first name. This is because you may be slow to react if someone calls you by a name other than your real name. But my only training

46

for this type of undercover mission was having watched all the James Bond movies.

After they had searched my room, I guess they were satisfied with who I was. Soon afterward, I was contacted. I received a call and was told to be in the parking lot at 4:00 a.m. the next morning. I almost called the whole thing off at that point. I hate to get up early.

I was out in the parking lot at 4:00 the next morning and this Jamaican dude, dreadlocks and all, picked me up in a small car. He said he was told to drive me out to the dirt airstrip, which was on the other side of the island. The reason we were leaving so early was to arrive at the airstrip just at daylight, check it out, and be gone to avoid running into any Jamaican police air patrols.

This driver almost killed me several times as we drove across the island. This part of Jamaica was mountainous and the roads were very narrow and curvy. He was driving extremely fast, and as we wound around the mountains, there were times we were only a few feet away from the edge of cliffs that dropped thousands of feet. There were no guardrails, and sometimes I saw rocks flying off of the cliffs behind us. When he got to a particularly narrow curve, he would blow his horn before taking it to warn people walking to get out of the way. We would come around the curve and there would be people hugging the wall of the mountain.

Now this was all bad enough, but somewhere about halfway through the trip, the guy decided to smoke the biggest joint of marijuana I'd ever seen. It looked like a Cuban cigar. He offered me one, but I told him no—the company I flew for required me to have blood tests. This was true, but the company I worked for was not the airline he assumed. Of course it didn't really matter that I turned him down because the car was soon filled with smoke. It reminded me of a Cheech and Chong movie that I had once seen.

The thought entered my mind that we could fly off the cliff in this small car. But, after a few minutes, for some odd reason, I began to relax. We stopped a short distance from the airstrip and picked up another individual. He was rather large and wore army fatigues. I had considered that if things went bad, I would have no trouble overtaking this stoned Jamaican driver. With the addition of this new, oversized passenger, I wasn't as confident.

47

We were now going slowly up a gully-filled dirt road with jungle vegetation scraping the sides of the car. Suddenly, we stopped and I was told to get out of the car. I got out and looked around and all I could see was jungle. Then, about fifty feet down the road, another Jamaican walked out of the jungle holding a machete. Now it was three to one, and something flashed through my mind that I had heard during the briefing before I took this mission. This group of smugglers had once beheaded a narcotics officer, put his head into a bale of marijuana, and left it on the doorstep of the police headquarters.

I had been training a great deal in karate, and I was working on my black belt. I was also pumping iron, bench pressing two hundred pounds for ten reps at a time, so I had been feeling invincible. That was before I was outnumbered three to one in the middle of the jungle with one person coming toward me with a machete. All I could do now was to assume a defensive stance and prepare for whatever happened.

When the Jamaican with the machete got about twenty steps away, I got a good look at him. His hair was long and in dreadlocks, and his eyes were frosted over. He looked evil, like the bad guy I had recently seen in a Steven Segal movie. Fortunately, when he got about ten steps away, he turned and disappeared into the jungle. I looked over at the driver and he just smiled and told me that this guy was the one who weeded the marijuana plants they had growing throughout the jungle.

We walked a short distance through the jungle and came out into a clearing that I discovered was the landing strip. They had bribed a local construction crew that was building a nearby road to let them use their equipment during the night to clear the jungle and build this landing strip. I walked the entire length of the strip to see if it was suitable for landing. Every five hundred feet, in the center of the strip, were several large holes.

When I questioned them about the holes they said that law enforcement authorities had discovered the strip and had blasted these holes, using dynamite, to make the airstrip unusable. They assured me they would fill in these holes the night before I was to land. They would do this the night before so as not to alert the authorities that we were going to use the field. They also told me they would drive a car at high speed up and down the runway to make sure it was smooth enough for me to land. Somehow, that was not too reassuring.

Since this airstrip was built into the side of a mountain, it was angled so one end was at least five hundred feet higher than the other. At the low end of the runway was a cliff that dropped off at least a thousand feet straight down. There would not be much room for error while landing or taking off.

They showed me an area off to the side of the runway where they had buried an airplane a few months before. It had landed to pick up the load of drugs, but then it would not start. Since they were worried about an air patrol spotting it, they quickly dug a large hole and buried this $250,000 airplane.

They also told me that at one time they were smuggling such a huge volume of drugs that one airplane would often have to circle overhead before landing because there was another airplane being loaded on this strip. They were buying aviation fuel from the Montego Bay Airport in such large quantities that they were told they were using more fuel than American Airlines.

I somehow managed to get back to my hotel room. I checked out and headed to the airport for the first flight off the island. Because they were watching me at the hotel I had not even had a chance to check in with my case agent. Customs hadn't heard from me in thirty-six hours and my agent was probably wondering if I was dead or just drinking rum on the beach.

As soon as I reached the airport, I went to a pay phone to call in. No sooner had I dialed than a Jamaican came over and picked up the phone next to me. There was a long row of phones that no one was using but he chose the one right next to me. I put the phone down and walked away. He did the same. He followed me around the airport, and I pretended I didn't see him. Every time I picked up a phone, he was close by. I managed to make a quick coded call to let my case agent know I was alive.

Finally, it was time to board the plane, and I'll be danged if he didn't get on the same flight. I connected flights in Miami to New Orleans and he got on that flight as well. There was now no doubt I was being tailed, but it wouldn't last long once we arrived in New Orleans.

When we got to New Orleans we were on my turf. My car was parked in the terminal garage, and I quickly departed the airport. Even if he had somehow managed to follow me, I knew that the streets in New Orleans are confusing. I made a few turns, and I was soon confident that no one could be following me. I could have had him detained by police, but I didn't want to blow the case.

A couple of weeks later, the drugs were ready for pickup in Jamaica, but we ran into some political problems. We had planned that I would pick up the drugs, fly them into Louisiana, and deliver them to Mr. Black's accomplices. That way, we could arrest the buyers and destroy their organization too. To do this, we had to get permission from the Jamaican government to fly the marijuana out of the country.

They refused, demanding instead that I pick up the drugs and then fly them to Kingston and turn them over to them. The customs special agent in charge (SAC) balked at this. Why risk my life to turn everything over to the Jamaicans—who would probably not arrest Mr. Black and might even end up selling the drugs themselves?

The undercover deal was falling apart fast, but I had an idea. I figured, why not call Mr. Black and ask him to come to New Orleans? I could tell him we needed to discuss some final details. It would be a hard sell, but if he fell for it, we could arrest him on conspiracy charges.

Days later, Mr. Black flew to New Orleans to meet me. I picked him up in my Mercedes Benz undercover car and drove him to my "office." My office was in a rented office building in downtown New Orleans that we used for undercover operations. It had hidden video recorders. Agents were standing by in a nearby office in case they were needed.

I had asked him to bring a sample of the marijuana I was picking up in Jamaica. He brought this to New Orleans, so now we could arrest him for possession as well as the conspiracy charges. This meeting went well, and I had him show me again on a map where the landing strip was located in Jamaica. We discussed all the other details of the smuggling venture. Of course, all this was captured on videotape.

I decided we had enough evidence to arrest him, but we didn't want to do it in our undercover office. It had taken a lot of time and money to set up the office, and we needed it for other cases. We got in my car, and I supposedly was driving him back to his hotel room. I told him I needed to pull into a gas station for a soda. This had been arranged, and there were a dozen or so customs special agents in plain clothes all around the station.

As soon as I got out of the car, making sure it was unlocked, the agents surrounded the car and arrested him. I can still remember the look on his face as he realized I was a cop—a look of disbelief and disappointment. It still haunts me some, because I had to befriend him. I had to do this mentally in order to pull off the undercover role. I had to convince myself I really was who I said I was, a smuggler and his friend.

You see in the movies how screwed up undercover cops get and you think it's just a movie plot, but let me tell you, working undercover really messes with your mind.

Mr. Black was sentenced to nine years in prison and a $300,000 fine, but his smuggling operation in Jamaica was probably only temporarily interrupted. There are always others waiting to take over. His main colleague, whom I met in Jamaica, was indicted, but Jamaican authorities would not extradite him. He was later arrested on a minor drug charge in rural Alabama. Before customs got word he had been arrested, he paid off the sheriff by buying him a new car and was released. He was never seen again in the United States.

I have to tell you a few other interesting things I learned while debriefing these two smugglers. At one time, Mr. X had his operation based out of the Cayman Islands. He rented a house there, figuring it was a pretty safe place to stay out of the spotlight of law enforcement. He told me that on one occasion he had the entire floor of one of his bedrooms stacked waist-high with money.

Money was coming in so fast that they stopped counting it. They had burned up two electric money counters so they just put money in a suitcase and weighed it. As long as the sum equaled within $50,000, give or take, of what they wanted it to be, it was close enough for their deals. Nobody was going to get upset over a measly fifty grand.

He also told me of another smuggling deal he did that went wrong. They had put three hundred thousand pounds—yes, three hundred thousand pounds—of marijuana into a barge and pushed it up the Mississippi River to Baton Rouge, Louisiana. If you have ever seen the Mississippi River, you know that there are barges constantly moving up and down the river. It is a very common sight, so they figured it would be the ideal way to smuggle. Who would suspect a barge was smuggling?

Well they were correct, no one did, and the barge made it to Baton Rouge. It was such a big load it required five eighteen-wheel trucks to move it off the barge. Since they wanted to do this quickly, they had the five trucks all ready and forty-five people to offload the marijuana. They paid them $50,000 each.

After they loaded the last truck, it would not start. They had no choice but to leave it on the dock, filled with marijuana. Naturally, it was not long before local police discovered it and the investigation led to arresting everyone in the offload crew. But that was days later. The main guy who had worked with Mr. X in setting up the deal got away. Mr. X told me that he made $17 million on this one deal.

The forty-five people in the offload crew all stood trial at the same time. Since there were so many of them, they held the trial in a high school gym. Most received probation with a big fine.

This smuggling venture had almost worked so well that Mr. X decided to try an even bigger load! They brought a barge to Colombia and loaded it with a million pounds of marijuana. This time, they were going to take it up the Mississippi River all the way to St. Louis. That was so far north that they hoped no one would ever suspect anyone of smuggling dope in a barge.

The barge was loaded, but problems arose with the ship pushing the barge, Colombian port police wanting some payoffs, and then stormy seas. Before they could set sail, the marijuana had started to rot in the hot hull of the barge. It smelled so bad that they knew they could never get past authorities along the Mississippi, so they called the whole thing off. I think this would have been the world's largest smuggling case.

During this time, Mr. Black even gave me his special recipe for his hashish oil. To smuggle this oil into Canada, he had designed a special form-fitting container that molded around the legs of the young women that he was using as smugglers. The container conformed to their body's shape, and customs officers would have had to strip search the women to find it. The women, young schoolteachers, would fly between Jamaica and Canada on regularly scheduled airliners, smuggling about three gallons at a time. They were paid $5,000 and given a free trip to Jamaica.

The marijuana Mr. Black smuggled out of Jamaica for Mr. X originated in Colombia. Jamaica was used as a pick-up point because airplanes could fly from there directly to the United States without refueling. Most planes couldn't do this from Colombia. Mr. Black, however, grew his own marijuana in Jamaica. It was a very potent variety that sold for five times the price of normal marijuana.

CHAPTER SEVEN

It was a training day, and I was assigned the Blackhawk. On training days, the branch stood down on normal operations and conducted training. We would do tactical training, such as handcuffing techniques, shooting at the range, air tactics, or whatever. On this day we were doing survival training.

Since we flew over oceans, mountains, deserts, and jungles, we had to be prepared to survive in any environment. Customs hired the best survivalists it could find to train us. For instance, the guy who taught us mountain survival had climbed Mt. McKinley (the highest mountain in North America) five times.

On this day, we were going to simulate a plane crash on a remote island. The pilots would have to survive until help arrived, which could be several days. I was assigned to fly the Blackhawk, so my job was to drop off five pilots and air officers to one of the barrier islands off of eastern Louisiana, called the Chandelier Islands. These islands were no more than a tiny strip of beach, but there were a few places you could land a helicopter. I dropped them off and they were supposed to build a shelter and prepare to be stranded there for a long time. Of course, I was going to pick them up later in the day.

No sooner had I landed back at the branch than we got a call from the Office of Investigations for some help. They had placed some agents on an oil rig deep in the Gulf of Mexico to watch for a shrimp boat. They had received information that a boat would dock at this abandoned rig and offload a load of dope to some fishing boats. The agents had been there a few days and were supposed to be picked up by a customs boat. But now a storm had popped up and the seas were too high for the customs boat to do the pickup. If this storm developed into a hurricane, the agents would be in trouble on this small, broken-down oil rig.

Therefore, the Office of Investigations wanted customs to send the Blackhawk to get the agents. I had to fly out to the island and pick up our pilots first and then come back and refuel. By the time I was headed out to the rig, the weather had deteriorated badly. The wind was already blowing at more than thirty miles per hour and it looked like the storm was going to get worse in a hurry. Any other time I would have turned back, but those guys were depending on me to get them off the rig.

I finally got to the rig and realized that the heliport was too small for the Blackhawk to land. The heliport was a small rectangular pad on top of the rig, surrounded by a tall wire fence. I just could not angle the Blackhawk into the pad without hitting the tail rotor on the fence. That was not my only problem—there was a wire cable lying across the pad that looked like it might fly up into the main rotor blades. If that happened, we would surely crash.

The storm was getting worse, and I had to rescue these guys in a hurry. I managed to hover over the pad low enough that the agents could climb aboard with the help of another agent in the back of the helicopter. It took a while to get everyone on board, and I had a hard time holding the helicopter steady. I had to hold it perfectly still because the agents were under it. The winds had reached thirty-five miles per hour and my tail rotor was a few feet from hitting the fence. The cable lying across the pad was being blown up off the deck a few inches and could come flying up into the rotors at any second. My co-pilot kept yelling for everyone to hurry up.

Finally, everyone was aboard and I lifted off the rig. That was about as close as I like to get to tragedy. If you haven't figured it out by now, you will by the end of this book: my guardian angel is over nine feet tall and wields a flaming sword that makes Darth Vader's light saber look like a child's toy.

The agents were very grateful as I flew them back to their office in Gulfport, Mississippi. By the time I was back on the ground in New Orleans, I was mentally and physically exhausted. Little did I know that my day had just begun!

When I landed, I was told that the branch chief wanted me in his office ASAP. I figured it was to thank me for a job well done, maybe to let me go home early. Boy was I wrong. A fugitive on the US Marshals' most wanted list had been spotted in a small town in Alabama. The marshals had requested that we fly a team of them up there as soon as we could.

I looked at the chief for a second before I said anything. I was extremely tired and this was a very long trip. Unfortunately, I was one of only two King Air pilots working that day, and it takes two pilots to fly the King Air. I would have complained if I thought it would have helped, but I knew I would be wasting my breath. The only good thing about this trip was that my co-pilot was the same pilot I had been flying with all day in the Blackhawk. Misery loves company.

On the way to Alabama, the marshals filled me in on the story. Local police had recognized a fugitive from a poster and had followed him to a house in a remote area outside of town. This fugitive was considered armed and dangerous. He was also a black belt in karate. He was wanted for making and selling meth, a poor man's cocaine that was becoming very popular. Meth was usually made by amateur chemists in their homes. It was dangerous to make because it involved several chemicals that could blow up, and accidents had already happened across the country.

The county sheriff picked us up at the airport and took us to his office to make a plan for the arrest. The marshals were experts—so they said—at this kind of stuff, so they told us pilots to just stay at the sheriff's office while they went out to the house to arrest the fugitive. Normally, I would have insisted on being part of the operation, but it had been over twelve hours since I had started my day, and I was so tired I could hardly stand up. They took off and I hoped they'd finish the job quickly so we could get back home.

They were out at the house, which was several miles out of town, when we got a call at the office that the fugitive had been spotted not far from where we were. It would take too long for the sheriff and marshals to return. So, along with the other customs pilot and one deputy, I ran to the deputy's car and sped off to catch this guy.

I was about half-awake when all this happened. I grabbed my bulletproof vest and jumped into the front passenger seat of the sheriff's patrol car. The deputy took off speeding before I had even put on my seat belt. I was being tossed around the car and somehow got all tangled up putting on my vest and seat belt. I am sure that the deputy was wondering what kind of idiots he had with him. Federal agents …ha!

The deputy drove like a bat out of hell through town. We arrived just as another deputy was pulling the fugitive over. I jumped out of the sheriff's car and drew my weapon as I approached the fugitive, who was still in his vehicle. I shouted for him to show me his hands. He looked at me for a second, not moving. I could tell he was considering his options.

He looked around and saw the other cops and decided he had no choice but to give up. We had just gotten him out of the car and put handcuffs on him when the marshals arrived. As they looked over at the subdued fugitive, I couldn't help asking them if there was anything else they wanted us to do for them today. I could tell they didn't much like us mere pilots making this arrest. Too bad!

While they were at the fugitive's house they had discovered evidence that he was in the process of making more meth. So now we had to get a search warrant, in the middle of the night, and search the house. This took a couple of hours. We all went out to the house and stood around outside waiting for the warrant. The next day, we discovered that at the very spot where I had stood waiting, $40,000 in cash was buried. If only I had known.

Finally, we got the warrant and began the search. Back then, meth labs were new, so none of us realized the danger of entering a working lab. Breathing the chemicals could kill you. The gas mask hanging on the wall as we entered the basement was a good clue. I was the first one down into the basement, and we found the largest meth lab in Alabama history!

The marshals were now content to turn things over to the sheriff, and we were ready to fly home. A quick check of the weather showed a line of thunderstorms between us and New Orleans. I was already tired, and I sure didn't feel like fighting thunderstorms all the way home. I told the marshals we would be staying there for the night.

That day turned out to be one of my busiest days ever: I had possibly saved some agents from dying in a hurricane, arrested a man on the ten most wanted list, and seized the largest meth lab in Alabama history. Pretty good day!

These are just my stories—there were many other customs pilots who had similar adventures around the country and beyond our borders. One day, when I was off duty, the branch got called in to assist in serving an arrest warrant in a remote area of southern Mississippi. The wanted individual lived in a small house out in the woods. It had only a dirt road leading up to it, and there was no way a police car could get close without being spotted. It was too difficult and dangerous to approach through the woods, so they requested a helicopter.

The person we were after was wanted on weapons charges. He was suspected of converting rifles to fully automatic and selling them to drug dealers and a host of other unruly characters. He was one of these anti-American survivalist types and had been overheard bragging to his friends that he would not be taken alive.

The Alcohol Tobacco and Firearms (ATF) agents who were running this case arranged that our helicopter would hover low overhead while they moved up the dirt road in several vehicles. The helicopter crew would watch the house, and if anybody ran into the woods, the helicopter could direct the agents. Sure enough, as soon as the vehicles started up the dirt road, the suspect ran out of his back door, holding what appeared to be an automatic rifle.

He ran about one hundred yards into the woods and stopped on top of a small ridge. He lay down on his stomach behind a dirt bank and pointed his weapon in the direction of the agents. He laid out beside him several magazines filled with ammo. There was no doubt that he intended to shoot anyone coming after him, and he had the location and firepower to hold off a small army.

Luckily, the helicopter crew had spotted him just before the agents reached a position where he could fire on them. The pilot radioed down to the agents on the ground to warn them, but for some reason their radios did not work. The helicopter crew estimated that, in less than a minute, the agents would be ambushed, so they decided to hover over the suspect as low as possible and try to take a shot.

The air enforcement agent who was sitting in the "gunner's window" in the back of the Blackhawk stuck his AR 15 rifle out the window to line up a shot. The suspect looked up, saw the helicopter over him, and suddenly threw down his weapon. He then stood up with his hands raised.

Once we had him in handcuffs, we asked why he suddenly gave up. He told us that he had intended to shoot it out, thinking that he had a very good chance of escaping. But when he looked up and saw the machine gun sticking out the window of the helicopter, he knew he would be killed if he began firing. I guess he did not know his weapons as well as he thought, though, because there was no machine gun sticking out of the helicopter window, just an ordinary rifle.

Customs was still sending aircraft down-range to the Caribbean, to Mexico, and to Central and South America to try to stop smugglers flying out of Colombia. In the first months of those operations, a CHET crew based out of the Jacksonville branch had a close encounter of a dangerous kind. They were chasing an aircraft that had just dropped a load of drugs to a boat in the Caribbean. They were following it, trying to determine where the aircraft was returning to in hopes of enlisting the help of law enforcement officers there. This aircraft was headed into Venezuela.

About thirty miles offshore, the CHET was intercepted by a Venezuelan air force fighter jet. It made a quick pass in front of the custom aircraft to get the crew's attention. Then it came up beside our aircraft and signaled for the crew to follow. The CHET crew had not planned on flying into Venezuelan airspace, which extends twenty miles offshore. By their instruments, they were still in international airspace, so they had no intention of following the Venezuelan fighter to Venezuela.

They turned around to get farther away from Venezuela, but the fighter had other plans for them. The fighter pilot fired several volleys of tracer rounds a short distance in front of the CHET! The crew now had no choice—if they did not want to be shot down, they had to follow the fighter plane into Venezuela.

They were escorted into Venezuela and directed to land at a military base. When they landed and taxied onto a ramp, they were surrounded by soldiers pointing machine guns at them. By this time, the CHET crew had contacted our command center, based at Howard Air Force

Base in Panama City, Panama, and advised them of situation. High-ranking State Department officials were already on the phone to their Venezuelan counterparts. The speedy response meant that the pilots were treated well and released within hours. The stunt had all been a political warning to stay out of Venezuelan airspace. We can only guess what would have happened if the CHET crew had not been able to make that radio call.

Another customs crew operating the Citation in Mexico almost got shot down as well. They had followed a suspect airplane into northern Mexico. The plane had landed on a dirt strip. The customs crew was flying in formation with a Mexican King Air airplane that had nine PGR agents onboard. PGR is the Mexican equivalent to our FBI. Since we could not make an arrest in Mexico, we often worked with them.

The Citation circled overhead as the drug plane began offloading its drugs into a truck. The PGR King Air landed on the short dirt strip and taxied up to the airplane. But before the agents could get out of the airplane, they were ambushed by Mexican soldiers who had been hiding in nearby trees. With the camera on in the Citation above, the crew could clearly see the King Air being shot up, but there was nothing they could do. Someone on the ground ordered the Citation to land, but of course the crew knew they would be shot if they did. They estimated more than fifty Mexican soldiers were on the ground. Later, we discovered that all nine PGR agents had been killed.

The Citation crew now had to figure out how to get out of Mexico. Having the video tape of this massacre involving the Mexican military was like carrying around a time bomb. The Mexicans would probably do anything to stop this tape from getting into the wrong hands. Unfortunately, the plane did not have enough fuel to fly to the United States. Landing anywhere in Mexico could be fatal, depending on how widespread the military involvement was.

The crew got on the radio and coordinated a plan with the help of the American Embassy and other customs officials working in Mexico. They landed at a major Mexican airport and were immediately escorted onto an American Airlines jet and flown to the United States. Within minutes they were heading to the United States with the video tape of the shootout. They made it out of Mexico with no problem and the president of the United States was viewing the tape a few hours later.

It caused a major uproar that lasted about a week. The Mexicans supposedly arrested the Mexican general who was using Mexican troops to assist the drug cartels. It was rumored that he was executed. But a couple of years later, I was working out of Monterrey, Mexico and one of my crewmembers, who could read Spanish, was reading the newspaper. Believe it or not, that same general was in town on some type of business. It seems that the Mexican government just hid him away for a year or two and gave him his old job back.

You can't have hundreds of aircraft flying around engaged in the type of missions we were conducting without having some accidents. During my career, I remember about half a dozen fatal accidents. One of the first accidents in customs aviation involved a Blackhawk crashing into the ocean about thirty miles offshore from Miami. I don't want to dwell on negative things, but doing a dangerous job, bad things do happen. One person was killed in this accident and three survived. I later talked to one of the survivors about the accident and his story was pretty incredible.

The Blackhawk was chasing a "go fast" boat loaded with drugs. It had originated somewhere in the Bahamas and was attempting to smuggle its load into southern Florida. A customs boat had intercepted it just offshore of Miami but could not catch it. They called in the Blackhawk to assist them. The Blackhawk was flying very low over the water and it was nighttime. It is very easy to lose your depth perception flying over water at night, and the helicopter simply flew into the ocean.

According to the survivor, they hit the water and almost instantly flipped upside down. It was dark and they were all underwater. Everyone scrambled to get out. He and another officer were in the back of the helicopter, and he literally could not tell up from down or where the doors or windows were located. He felt around, trying to find a way out of the helicopter.

He was in this situation for what seemed like a long time, and he did not know if the helicopter was sinking. He was afraid he might be hundreds of feet underwater. Still he could not find a way out. Finally, after holding his breath as long as he could, he passed out. But instead of drowning, he floated up to the top, which was really the floor, and hit his head. This woke him up, and there was a small air pocket against the ceiling just big enough that he could take a breath of air.

He took a few breaths and again dived down to try to find a way out of the helicopter. Soon he passed out again trying to find the air pocket. Again, he floated up to the ceiling, hit his head, woke up, and found the air pocket. He does not remember how many times he passed out and was revived by hitting his head and finding the air.

By now he was sure he was deep under the ocean, but by some miracle, he finally found a way out of the helicopter. He swam to the surface and was relieved to find that he had only been about twenty feet underwater. The helicopter had enough trapped air inside that it was floating just beneath the surface.

The pilot never made it out of the helicopter. Before rescue divers could reach him, the helicopter sank into a twenty-five-hundred foot deep section of the ocean. A remote controlled submarine later confirmed that the pilot's body was still strapped into the pilot's seat. Due to the depth, it was impossible to recover him.

Less than a year after this accident, the New Orleans Blackhawk that I often flew crashed into the woods in Mississippi. The crew had chased a plane into a small airport and were hovering low around the perimeter, looking for possible offload crews, when they had a mechanical failure. They were forced to land in the middle of a group of pine trees. The rotor blades managed to chop down several trees, but, of course, the helicopter was destroyed. Luckily, my fellow pilots and air officers were unhurt. Also luckily, I was not flying that day.

Hurricane Andrew was heading toward the Miami Air Branch and I was ordered to go pick up one of their Blackhawks and fly it out of harm's way. All the Miami pilots were busy evacuating their families and boarding up their homes. I arrived at the branch, located at the Homestead Air Force Base, the day before the hurricane hit. Little did I know that the Air Branch, and most of Homestead, would soon be wiped out. I met with the branch chief, who was a former New Orleans pilot whom I knew well. He was a little upset that this hurricane was headed for his branch. He had only started as branch chief weeks earlier. What a way to start a new job.

I flew the Hawk to Jacksonville, the last flyable aircraft to leave the air branch. One Blackhawk was not flyable due to a maintenance problem and was secured in the hangar. During the storm the hangar fell on top of it and totally destroyed it.

Hurricane Andrew wasn't content on just crushing Florida, it continued on to hit southern Louisiana. The damage to Louisiana was nowhere near as bad as Florida but it did create a tornado that hit a small community just outside New Orleans.

The whole country was helping out the victims in Florida, so a few fund-raisers popped up in New Orleans to help the local victims too. I heard that the actor Steven Segal was going to be at a mall near my house as part of one of these fund-raisers. I already have mentioned to you that I loved karate at the time and Segal was my hero. He was the real deal and had a sixth-degree black belt. I really enjoyed his karate movies, *Out For Justice*, *Hard To Kill*, etc. His style of karate was very similar to the one I was studying.

Anyway, I was looking forward to meeting him. I arrived at the mall and they had an entire parking lot blocked off for the event because there were so many people. I followed the crowd and could barely see Segal at the front of a line of at least five hundred people. He was signing autographs.

I'm not much for waiting in line, so I followed the golden rule— "Those that have the gold, make the rules." I used my "gold badge" to break the line and walked right up to the front of the line. Segal was surrounded by a dozen sheriff's deputies. I approached the highest ranking deputy and showed him my badge. We work with these guys all the time, so they at least knew what a customs pilot was.

The deputy led me to the sheriff himself. The Jefferson Parish sheriff, Harry Lee, was a local legend. He had been sheriff for over twenty years and was on the news almost every night. He looked at me like, "What do you think you are doing?"

I had to think fast, so I told him I was a customs pilot and wondered if he and Segal would like to take a Blackhawk ride over the hurricane-damaged area. He grinned, grabbed my hand, pulled me to the head of the line and introduced me to Steven. Stevey, as Sheriff Lee called him, was excited about flying in a Blackhawk. He stopped the line and talked with me for several minutes. I think he was making sure I was someone he wanted to fly with. He introduced me to his wife at the time, actress Kelly LeBrock. I recognized her from her movies but honestly did not know they were married. I looked back at the line of people behind me. I'm sure they were wondering who I was and why I had stopped the line.

We set it all up to fly the next day. I was to pick up Segal, his wife, and the sheriff at the Superdome Stadium heliport. Now I just had one small problem—I did not have permission to fly them. For some reason that I just can't figure out, I was not allowed to fly whomever I wanted, whenever I wanted, in the $17 million Blackhawk. Government regulations, what a pain!

I called my supervisor and filled him in on how the sheriff had requested the Blackhawk to survey the hurricane damage. I convinced him that this would be great for public relations. The public would appreciate us helping Segal raise money for those poor people who had lost their homes. He agreed to the flight, but he thought it would be a good idea if some of the NO SHIT team was along on the flight. And oh, by the way, a supervisor should come along to make sure everything went right. I was beginning to wonder if I was going to have room for Segal.

I landed at the Superdome heliport the next day. Segal showed up in a motorcade that equaled some I had seen escorting the president of the United States. There had to be ten sheriff's vehicles. I found out quickly that Steven and the sheriff were big friends. But I'll give credit where credit is due—Segal was number one at the box office at the time.

I had six agents with me. We were all wearing black fatigues and were heavily armed. Steven pushed through the crowd, shook my hand, and acted like we were old buddies. Kelly was very nice and friendly. She was as beautiful in person as she was on screen.

I put her and Steven in the open "gunner's window" of the Hawk and we took off. We were so loaded with people, I was worried about taking off. But as my grandfather used to say, "Don't worry about the mule, just load the wagon!"

We made a few low passes around the French Quarter and the Riverwalk of New Orleans and headed out to look at the houses destroyed by the hurricane. After we had done that, I began giving them a low, high-speed tour of the Louisiana swamps. That lasted until the sheriff said he'd had enough and asked me to take him back. He was getting airsick.

We landed at the New Orleans airport so Steven and Kelly could catch their flight back home. They made a great couple, and I was shocked when I heard later they were breaking up. Before they departed, they posed for pictures. I know they get tired of that, but I guess that's the price of fame.

This was not the only time I would meet Steven. This introduction to US Customs had stirred his interest. He was a law enforcement enthusiast and collected badges. Not only was he into karate, but he loved to shoot weapons of all kinds, and told me he shot over a thousand rounds per month. That's more than we shot as elite SRT team members. He was very pro-law enforcement, and the sheriff had made him an honorary deputy sheriff. He wanted a customs badge.

The special agent in charge (SAC) in New Orleans required him to go through a three-day training class given to local and state officers before they work on customs cases. I figured he would never go for that, but surprisingly, he agreed. A few months later, he attended the class and was given a badge. No authority of course, just an honorary badge.

He gave a party afterward in his hotel suite and invited me. There were lots of people, but he was a good host. He asked a lot of questions about our SRT team and wanted to get in on some real police action. Later, I ran this by the branch chief, who thought I was crazy for asking. For some reason he thought it would be bad press if Segal got killed working on a dangerous mission with us. I didn't see a problem, but he was the boss.

Later the US Customs national PR guy in D.C. contacted Steven and asked him to do a poster for customs to help in the drug war. A kind of, "Don't smuggle drugs; no one's above the law" type of poster.

He agreed, and a nationwide contest within customs was launched to come up with the best slogan. Then something happened that I'm still mad about. A negative magazine article came out about Segal. He was depicted as the bad boy of Hollywood. It caused such a stir that customs decided to drop him and the national poster campaign.

Here we had a big movie star willing to do this public relations project for free, something that might really help deter some people from using drugs, and we just said, "sorry, we don't need you anymore." I think Steven was also mad about this, and I don't blame him. I never heard from him again.

CHAPTER EIGHT

Soon after the success of the Jamaican caper, I was asked by the Office of Investigations to do another undercover mission. This one would turn out to be an even greater adventure and a lot more dangerous.

This time, the target was a major smuggling organization working out of Belize in Central America. This group was responsible for smuggling hundreds of thousands of pounds of marijuana and cocaine into the United States. The brains behind this organization was a local Belizean, and it was thought that if we could capture him it would end the whole smuggling ring.

The man, whom I will call "John," was already wanted in the United States on several charges, but Belize would not extradite him. So basically, he could operate freely as long as he stayed in Belize. My job was to fly to Belize, again posing as a pilot, set up a smuggling deal, and somehow manage to get him to fly out of Belize with me. Then we could arrest him. Simple, right?

I had a little help. We had a man living in New Orleans who used to live in Belize. Since Belize is a very small country, he knew John. If we paid him the right amount of money, he would introduce me to John.

We flew down to Belize in a Piper Navajo, which is a mid-sized twin engine airplane. It required only one pilot, so it was perfect for the trip. This particular plane had been seized from a smuggler a few years prior, so it not only looked like a smuggler's airplane, it was one! It had extra long-range fuel tanks, so I could fly from New Orleans direct to Belize City, if the winds and weather were good, and if I went direct. I mention direct because that required me to fly over the Yucatan Peninsula of Mexico.

Flying over another country in a US "government" aircraft required permission from that country. Due to the corruption in Mexico, if I had gotten permission, then the wrong people in Belize would have known who I was before I even landed. Since the plane I was flying had a fake registration number, and since I was on a flight plan with a fake name and I was not spying on Mexico, it seemed reasonable to just fly over Mexico. After all, stopping the flow of drugs is in Mexico's best interest too, right?

We landed in Belize City and I ran into trouble right away. I had asked our maintenance department before I departed to sanitize the airplane. This means that they should go through the plane and remove anything that would indicate that it was a government airplane. I followed this with my own check, but I failed to recognize that they took out the door keys.

The Navajo has wing lockers, a type of baggage area located in the wings. These are locked in flight to prevent them from accidentally opening. When we landed we had to be searched by Belize customs officials, and when they asked to look in these wing baggage lockers, I didn't have a key.

Here we were in this airplane that was commonly used by smugglers, and we were dressed to look like smugglers, and now I couldn't provide access to the airplane baggage area. It would look suspicious to me, and I'm sure it looked suspicious to the agent as well. He wasn't buying that I had forgotten the keys. If he started checking and found the airplane was not even registered, I would really be in trouble. At the very least, it would blow my cover.

I pulled my buddy, the man from Belize, to the side and pulled out some cash. I told him to try and pay this customs guy off so we could get on our way. I didn't want to do it myself and end up in jail for bribing an official. But as I said before, money is the universal language, and we were soon cleared to enter the country.

We got a room and called John. We set up a meeting for 10 p.m. at a little park on the ocean front that was near the hotel. Then I covertly met with two DEA agents who were working out of the American Embassy. They were to be my backup while in country. They set up a listening device on a rooftop overlooking our meeting area. They would record the meeting, and if I got into any trouble, they would be there to help me, I hoped.

They briefed me on what they knew about John and his smuggling organization. The part that interested me most was about how violent John supposedly was. Several people who were associated with him had disappeared in the jungle. It was highly suspected that he killed anyone who crossed him. I was wondering why I was only hearing about these things once I was already committed. But what the hey, it was just a meeting in town and several agents would be watching. How dangerous could that be?

John was right on time for our meeting. I am kind of a history buff, and I had read about how the Mayan civilization had mysteriously disappeared. When I saw John for the first time, I knew that this was a myth. John looked exactly like a Mayan was supposed to look. He looked just like a carving from an old Mayan ruin. Later, I found out he was from an Indian tribe, which undoubtedly directly descended from the ancient Mayans.

The first thing he wanted to do, after our introductions, was to get in his car for a little trip. The DEA agents, who were watching me from the roof, had told me not to leave the area. They would be unable to provide any security if I did. But I did not want to come this far and blow the case, so I got in the car.

Belize City is a small town, and it wasn't long until we were leaving the city and entering the jungle. It was nighttime and there were no street lights, so it was extremely dark. The roadway turned into a small two-lane, pothole-filled, poor excuse for a highway, and I began to think I should have listened to the DEA agents and not gotten into this car. The stories of the people disappearing in the jungle entered my mind.

We stopped at this bar about ten miles out of town. It was located on the beach and would have been a really cool place under any other circumstances. The bar was almost deserted, and we got a table off to the side. I guess John was comfortable there, and I'm sure he had people watching to make sure he was not followed.

He immediately liked me and was very interested in setting up a smuggling deal. I guess I must look like a smuggler. He talked for twenty minutes about how many pilots he had made rich. I wondered to myself why he needed another pilot if so many were making so much money. My pay was going to be $250,000. Now, I know where all the radar coverage is across the southern United States. I know where and when customs aircraft are patrolling. In short, I could run this load with a high chance of being successful. Customs would never know, right?

I was only tempted for a few seconds. I've worked in prisons. When I was a military policeman, I worked a great deal in a military stockade. My senior year of college at Middle Tennessee State University I worked as a prison guard at the Tennessee State Prison. I know for a fact that I'm just not the kind of person who would do well in prison. But when you think about it, who is?

We broke up this meeting, and on the way back to town John asked me to meet a friend of his who was coming in from Colombia in a couple of days. He promised it would be worth it.

After he dropped us off, I had another secret meeting with DEA. They were not happy at all that I had gotten into the car. I think they were more worried about covering their butts if anything happened to me on their watch than the case. I don't blame them. They have a tough job and there's always a fine line to walk while determining when a case is too dangerous to continue.

The way I looked at it, if you don't take a few chances, you never will make a case. Disbanding this smuggling organization might save a hundred lives back in the United States, not to mention the millions of dollars in direct and indirect cost of a drug-filled society. Whether you know it or not, every time you buy a product, there is an extra cost involved because of the security needed against dope-head thieves and shoplifters, workers who miss work because of drug problems, drug induced manufacturing screw-ups, police protection, and emergency room costs. I could go on, but you get the point.

Illegal drugs cost us all a great deal of money and heartache. Almost everyone knows someone who has had problems, either medically or legally, with drugs. I took my job seriously, and there was not enough money in the world to keep me from doing all I could do to stop illegal drugs from entering the United States. But, I would rethink that last statement when I met John's friend two days later!

My new Belizean friend and I had a day off before we had our next meeting, so I wanted to visit a nearby Mayan ruin. We hired a cab to drive us about fifteen miles out of town to the ruins. We were the only ones there. The ruins were very impressive. On the top of one temple was a round table-like stone where human sacrifices were made by the Mayans. I lay down on it and had my picture taken.

Next, we decided to look inside one of the large stone structures. There were no doors, but there was a cave-like entrance to somewhere, so we walked in. It quickly got dark and scary, and I had no flashlight, so we turned around. When we headed back out into the light, I could see I had walked under the largest wasps' nest I had ever seen in my life. It had been on the ceiling, not two feet over my head. I'm allergic to wasp stings, and we were a long way from medical help.

There was only one way out, and it was directly below this nest! Oh well, if they had wanted to sting us they would have gotten us on the way in, right? Anyway, that is what I told myself and my partner. I believe he would have been content to live the rest of his life right where he was instead of walking past that nest.

I guess you know I made it out alive, or you wouldn't be reading about it. I guess I never learn, because I got myself into two other similar situations during my later travels. I was at another Mayan ruin outside of Meridia, Mexico. I had climbed up to the top of a large pyramid. At the top was an opening where the Mayan priest once lived or worshiped. I walked into this chamber and heard this loud humming noise. I looked up. The entire ceiling and most of the walls were covered with bees. I quickly exited out the other side of the chamber, which was the fastest way out. On the entrance to this side was a large sign. It read "Danger African killer bees—Do not enter." Nice of them to put the sign on only one side.

The other time, I was crawling through an "off the beaten path" pyramid near Memphis, Egypt. I had already climbed inside the Great Pyramid of Giza but wanted to get away from the normal tourist attractions. It was cool seeing places that were relatively unchanged since they were found. There were few other tourists and I felt a little like Indiana Jones. After I was finished exploring inside the pyramid, the guide asked me if I had seen the cobra. Apparently, a large cobra lived inside that they had been trying to kill for some time! Why do I always seem to find these things out after the fact?

We returned to the Belize mission. After dinner my new "Belizean friend" wanted to take me to some bars he knew. He seemed to know everyone, and they were all curious about who this white American was who was with him. I think my friend was a little more involved in the smuggling trade than I was led to believe. As soon as they discovered I was a pilot, I was propositioned several different times to fly marijuana back to the States. Was everyone in Belize a smuggler? I could have made a dozen cases, but I had to remain focused on my primary mission.

The next day, John called us at our hotel and requested that we meet at the place of our first visit. We caught a cab, but before he took us to our meeting, we had to pay half in advance so he could stop and buy enough gas to get us there. The taxi was an unidentifiable model, made up of pieces from several types of vehicles. Beggars can't be choosers, so off we went. When we were almost there, the driver turned off the highway on to a dirt road leading up to the bar. Suddenly, there was this loud thump and the taxi ran off into the ditch beside the road. Luckily, we had been traveling only twenty miles per hour, so no one was injured. I got out and checked the damage. One of the wheels had broken off the cab! If this would have happened moments earlier when we were going sixty on the narrow highway, well …

John's friend was a Colombian who was trying to smuggle large amounts of cocaine into the United States. He asked me if I had any problems with moving cocaine. I had discovered both here and in Jamaica that some smugglers thought it was morally wrong to smuggle cocaine. Marijuana, on the other hand, was a natural herb, good for you in a lot of ways. It should not be illegal, at least in their minds.

I told him I was in this for the money. Dope was dope as far as I was concerned, but cocaine carried a lot stiffer jail sentence and would cost him. He just grinned. It was exactly what he expected to hear.

This was during the time Pablo Escobar, of the Medellin Cartel fame, was the number one smuggler in the world. A big manhunt was underway for him in Colombia. This man worked for another cartel and was a little upset about all the attention Escobar was getting in Colombia. Little did he know that I was heavily involved in the search for Escobar, but that's another story you'll hear later.

Again, he was an interesting target, but I had to finish what I had come to do, and that was to get John out of the country. I told him that, after I finished my business with John, I would work his deal. To make sure I wouldn't forget him, he said he would pay me $1 million dollars per load! This time it took me a whole ten seconds to remember I was not really a smuggler.

The Colombian finally departed, and I got down to the real business with John. I told him I could easily smuggle into the United States, that I was the pilot for a small company, and if I told them I was taking the airplane to Louisiana for maintenance, I could use it to run a load. I knew about a small airport in a rural area that I could use in the middle of the night that was safe. The airport manager was my friend, and even if I had trouble with an unexpected arrival of a sheriff's patrol, he could take care of it. I had him convinced he could trust me, so I put my plan into action.

I told him that I was comfortable smuggling the load into the United States, but once it got there I didn't have any way of storing it or selling it. What I needed was for him to assure me that, once I landed, he would have someone trustworthy pick up the dope at the airport. I dropped a few more hints. I knew that he was afraid to make phone calls to the United States and I was hoping that he would volunteer to fly back with me to set things up in person. I knew it had to be his idea, or he would be suspicious. After I kept on about being nervous about getting rid of the dope once I landed, he finally said, "What if I fly back with you to set things up?"

Yes! The plan was coming together. But I didn't want to appear too anxious. I said there was some risk to me to be smuggling him into the country illegally. He agreed and offered me $5,000 to do it. I almost laughed. Did I forget to tell you I was wired? Everything he said was being recorded. This was very dangerous to do. If he found the wire on me, it would be bad. However, the American ambassador, who was working with customs on this undercover operation, had insisted that if we did not have proof that John had departed Belize of his own free will, it would be considered kidnapping by the Belizean government.

Now, you may think this is a lot of bull hockey, and so did I at first. To me, it would have been a lot simpler to knock John on the head, throw him in the plane, and fly him away. But the United States is a nation of laws. On cases like this, they give the undercover operative a lot of discretion, as long as we follow the rules. If we were to start acting in an uncivilized way, it would create all sorts of international problems, affecting much larger cases in the United States and around the world. And that was the trick I learned by working some of our nation's biggest undercover cases. It was easy to catch a bad guy. But to do it in a way that would hold up in a court of law was quite another thing. Sometimes the laws favored the bad guy.

CHAPTER NINE

John said he had to wrap up a few things before he left, so we decided that I would pick him up two days later on a little barrier island just off the coast. There was a small unmanned airport there, and I was to land, leaving the engines running, and he would climb aboard. We agreed to meet again the next night—the night before the flight—to make the final arrangements. John left the bar.

My cohort and I got up to leave, and we realized that we did not have a ride back to town. The bartender said that taxis would not pick up fares this far out. He told us to walk out to the highway, where we could soon catch a bus back to town.

Now, in the movies you see those buses in foreign countries that are filled with the locals carrying goats and chickens into the city. That's all Hollywood stuff, right? You would be wrong. The bus that picked us up was just like that, except I think there was a pig in there, too. It was a long ride into town.

The next night, John did not call at the time he was supposed to. This worried me. He had been anxious the day before about flying to the States. At every meeting and phone call with him up to now, John had been right on time. I got the feeling that something was wrong.

I contacted the DEA, whose agents were still covertly watching my back, to see if they knew John's whereabouts. They didn't, but they agreed that something was wrong. We were supposed to fly in the morning. I wondered if somehow John had been tipped off, and I started asking the DEA agents some questions. I didn't like the answers.

To avoid being accused of kidnapping John and causing an international incident, they had decided to let their Belize law enforcement counterparts know about the undercover operation. I found out that as many as twenty people inside the Belize government now knew about this. My Belizean friend, who had introduced me to John, had already warned me that John was paying off some officials inside the government. I was sure that this was true—how else to explain his ability to operate so openly in this country?

We were getting a bad feeling that John had indeed been tipped off. My friend was scared to death. He was certain that John would send someone to our hotel during the night to kill us. The DEA offered us a safe house to spend the night. We could not fly out of Belize until daylight. It was illegal to fly in Belize at night and the airplane was locked up at the airport.

We had no choice but to stay the night. Maybe we were just imagining all of this. There could be another reason John had disappeared. I decided to just stay at the hotel. The agents could stay up all night and watch out for me. I put a chair against the door and tried to get some sleep. It didn't come.

Believe it or not, John called me in the middle of the night. He had wanted to party on his last night in Belize, so he had visited his favorite whore house and had gotten a little drunk. I wondered what the world was coming to when you couldn't even depend on a scumbag smuggler to be on time anymore.

Everything was set to pick up John at 10:00 the next morning at this small airstrip on the barrier island. I made a call to the case agent, who started calling all the people in customs and the American Embassy in Belize that had to give their final approval. I would leave all the bureaucratic crap to them. I went to sleep.

I woke up the next morning in a good mood. My plan was coming together perfectly. We were about to capture one of the biggest smugglers of all time. I packed up my luggage and was just about to walk out of my hotel room when the phone rang. I wish I had not answered it.

A Customs Office of Investigations supervisor was on the line, and he told me that deal was off. I could not believe it! He said that the American ambassador to Belize had determined that the Belizean government would consider this kidnapping. I explained to the supervisor that I had John on tape not only requesting to go with me, but offering to pay $5,000 to do it. He understood, but he said that all of this was way beyond his pay grade. The decision had been made, and all I could do was make the best of it.

He wanted me to go ahead and fly out to the island and meet John, and then to come up with some excuse as to why we could not fly him today. He suggested that there was a chance that the ambassador would change his mind, and this left open the possibility that we could fly John another day. I don't think management appreciated the position it put me in. John could take this very badly. It had taken days to build up his trust, and it was no small commitment on his part to travel into the United States. Now I was supposed to just fly out there and tell him the trip was off?

My Belizean counterpart and I flew out to the island to meet John. The airstrip's runway was so narrow that the wheels of my airplane had only inches on each side. Now, normally this would not create a major problem, but that day there was a very strong crosswind. This made the landing about a nine on a scale of ten in difficulty. I'm telling you, nothing is simple!

I somehow managed to land the airplane, and I taxied down to the end of the runway. There was John with a grin on his face, a piece of luggage in his hand, and $5,000 dollars in his pocket. We were that close to getting him! The thought ran through my mind to go ahead and allow him on the plane. But I knew that if I did that, he would not be the only one arrested when I landed in New Orleans.

I shut down the engines, got out of the airplane, and walked up to John. I told him I had just found out that customs was working a major operation in the area that I intended to land in the United States and that it was not safe to fly him today. I was sorry, but I was just looking out for him. I said that I knew that he didn't want any problems in the States, so we would have to do this another day. He didn't look too pleased, but he said, "Okay," and he walked away.

I flew back to the main airport in Belize City and was met by the DEA agents. They told me that they had received word for me to fly back to the States. The customs special agent in charge had determined it would be too dangerous for me to hang around while waiting for a political decision. That was fine with me. I was discouraged, angry, and ready to just go home. Over the last few days, I had risked my life for nothing. I flew back to New Orleans thinking that this case was over for good. Little did I know that I would be making one more trip to Belize!

When we landed on American soil, my Belizean friend got out of the airplane and kissed the ground. I guess he really had been frightened. Customs ended up paying him a lot of money for his role in introducing me to John. I got a "thank you, and oh, by the way, can you come in to work early tomorrow?"

When I got back to the office, everyone was disappointed that we had come so close and not been able to capture John. We discussed this for several days, trying to figure out alternative ways to capture him. Then we got the final word from the American Embassy in Belize that we could not fly John out of the country.

Everyone was resigned to the fact that the case was over. But I said, "If it is over, what do we have to lose if I just call John on the phone and continue with the smuggling deal we had set up?" We could not get John to the United States, but maybe we could force the police authorities in Belize to arrest him. We could also arrest the people in the United States with whom John had arranged to pick up the drugs.

I called John and—believe it or not—he was still eager to do the drug deal. To make sure that everything was coordinated on the American side, as I kept insisting, he was going to send his son to America. I was to pick up his son at the New Orleans airport and fly him to Atlanta to meet with the person to whom I was to deliver the drugs. All of a sudden, this case was back on, big time.

A few days later, I picked up John's son at the airport and checked him into a hotel near Slidell, a small town north of New Orleans. This was where the small airport was located that I was going to use in the smuggling operation. We worked out a plan to fly to the Stone Mountain Airport in Georgia the next day to meet with the individual to whom John was selling the marijuana.

I was busy with other customs work, so in order to save time flying on this long trip, I decided to take a King Air instead of the Navajo. The King Air is a much larger airplane than the Navajo, but also much faster. This decision almost blew the case. The Stone Mountain Airport was located just east of Atlanta. There is actually a mountain made of stone there, in the middle of the big flat delta. It looks very much out of place and is kind of a tourist attraction.

The Stone Mountain Airport had a very short runway. I'm not sure that anyone had ever landed a King Air there before; when I taxied onto the ramp a lot of people were looking at me kind of strangely. So much for keeping a low profile!

The person we were meeting walked out to the airplane, and we all sat inside and had our discussion. This was all planned, of course, because the airplane was wired with a recording device. We worked out the final details on how and when he was to meet me and pick up the thousand pounds of marijuana I was flying into the country.

Before he departed, he asked me why we were flying in an army airplane. This man knew something about airplanes. The King Air I was flying was an old army surplus airplane they called a C-12. It had no markings or anything else that would distinguish it from a normal civilian airplane, except that the army had put the landing lights in a different place. Few people would be aware of this difference, but somehow, this man knew.

It turned out that he had worked at an army base. I knew that he was not too concerned or he would not have agreed to the deal. I told him that the army sold these aircraft as surplus, and a lot of civilian companies flew them. He seemed satisfied with the answer.

A couple of days later, I took off to Belize to pick up the dope. I was supposed to land at daybreak at the same island airstrip where I had met John earlier. I had to refuel in Belize City before landing on the island, so that I would have enough fuel for my return trip. Since flying in Belize is illegal at night, I had to get there before dark, spend the night, and then fly to the island at daybreak.

The DEA agents had me park in a special place at the airport, where they had access. That way, I could get into the airport the following morning before the airport was open and take off. I needed to take off while it was still dark in order to arrive at the island at sunrise. John had said that they needed to load the marijuana into my plane early, before anyone was up. The agents told me not to worry, they had arranged everything with the airport authorities. If everything went right, John would think that I had flown to the island directly from New Orleans.

I got a little sleep and the DEA agents picked me up before dawn. Why do these things always have to start so early? They drove me to the airport and used their key to get inside the large fence that surrounded the airport. I started up the airplane and taxied out to the runway. It was still dark, and the control tower was still closed.

I arrived at the small airstrip just at sunrise and could just barely make out the narrow, unlit runway. Of course, the wind was a direct crosswind, and this time it was even stronger than before. Have I mentioned that nothing is ever easy? I managed to land once again, and I parked the airplane at the end of the runway, as I had been directed. I turned off the engines and got out. I looked around. No one was there!

This was supposed to be a fast land, load, and takeoff. Something was wrong. Of course it was. What had gone right with this case yet? After about five minutes, a man approached. He said he worked for John. He had the marijuana in a boat, but he couldn't bring it to the plane because there were police on the island. I looked over at the nearby marina, and I saw at least fifty boats. The man told me that John had said I should contact him later, but the deal was off for now.

There was nothing I could do, so I got into the airplane and flew back to Belize City to advise the DEA of the situation. Maybe they would search the boats. This case was now officially a goat rope in my book, and I was through screwing around with it.

I found out later that the DEA and Belize officials had covertly placed a law enforcement tactical team on the island during the night. They were hiding in the jungle and watching the airport runway. They weren't as covert as they thought they were, it seems, since the smugglers had spotted them. The DEA should have told me about this. It could have gotten me killed!

I landed at the Belize City airport and started to taxi over to where the DEA agents were supposed to meet me. The control tower ordered me, not very kindly, to instead taxi to the base of the control tower. This was not good; I knew they were not happy about something.

I was busy shutting off my engines and turning off everything in the cockpit when I looked up to see two angry-looking police officers pointing automatic rifles at me. They yelled for me to get out of the airplane. I was actually not too worried at this point; I still thought that the DEA had everything taken care of. To be honest, there was one small thing that did have me a little concerned. I was not supposed to be armed in a foreign country, but that morning, before I had taken off, one of the DEA agents had insisted that I take the pistol he gave me. That was just in case things went badly at the drug pick-up.

If the Belize authorities found me with this gun, I would be in big trouble, undercover agent or not. I managed to stick it behind some radios in the cockpit without them seeing me, I hoped. I got out of the plane, and they told me to follow them to the "captain's office." The captain was the head of airport security. I was escorted to his office as if I was the world's biggest criminal.

When I arrived at the office, I was told to sit down. The captain immediately started drilling me. "Why did you take off before daylight? How did you get to your airplane? Where did you go?" Before I could answer any of the questions, he yelled, "You're under arrest!" Then he went over and picked up the phone and told someone to seize my airplane.

I had been told before this mission began that some Belize officials were corrupt—some even worked for the smugglers. It was reported that they often put people in jail for extended periods without filing any reports. Some people just vanished.

So, now I didn't know if I should tell him who I was or play dumb in hopes that the DEA agents would soon arrive. I decided to keep my cover a while longer. After about thirty minutes, I was beginning to worry that they were about to take me to jail or shoot me. It was getting very intense!

Finally, the DEA agents arrived. One of them knew the captain and told him who I was. The captain asked me why I hadn't just told him in the first place. I didn't really want to tell him that it was because I thought he was corrupt. I just laughed and said, "And, what, miss all this fun?"

The captain escorted me down to my airplane. I got in and started the engines. I was very ready to get out of this place! I radioed the control tower for takeoff instructions, and they told me to shut off my engines and come back inside. Out of my cockpit window, I could see the DEA agents leaving in their car.

The airport authorities had forgotten to collect all the airport fees from me. I was sure that they were making these fees up, but I paid them anyway. I just wanted to leave. Besides, it wasn't my money. By the time I was back at the plane, I had paid out over $400 in cash.

The flight back to New Orleans was problematic. I was in such a rush to take off that I did not refuel the airplane or check the weather reports. My early morning flights back and forth to the island had burned about an hour of fuel. The trip back to the Belle Chase Navy Base took me over the Yucatan Peninsula of Mexico and over seven hundred miles of ocean.

I would be crossing the furthest points between land in the Gulf of Mexico. I had estimated that, with full tanks, I would have an hour and a half of fuel reserve. But now an hour of my reserve fuel was already gone. That left me with only thirty minutes of extra fuel. If I encountered any headwinds, it was very likely that I would not have enough fuel to complete the trip. Not having had a chance to check the weather forecast, I had no idea if I would encounter headwinds or not.

I figured that I would make the decision on crossing the Gulf of Mexico once I reached Merida. Once I was airborne, though, I remembered that I could not land in Mexico because I was not even supposed to be in Mexico. I looked at my map and decided that Key West, Florida would be my alternate. Of course, if I landed there, I would probably be arrested again. I was in an airplane commonly used for smuggling, with no seats in the back, with a fake registration number, and I had only fake ID. Key West, because of its location, was one of those airports that were watched closely by law enforcement. Oh well, I was beginning to like being arrested.

I had just crossed over Merida and was entering the Gulf when I decided to call for a winds and weather check. I wanted to be out of Mexico and in international airspace in case I was asked for my location. Then I discovered yet another problem! Was this case cursed? The airplane's radio speaker system had stopped working. I could transmit out on the radios but could not hear a reply.

This would not have been a problem if I had a headset. But all of the headsets had "US Customs" stamped on them, so I had left them behind. Now I could not check the winds. Not only was that a problem, but what if there were bad thunderstorms in Louisiana? Even if I did have enough fuel to reach Belle Chasse, maybe the airport would be closed due to weather. Also, I'd have to communicate with air traffic control to enter the United States or land at a navy base.

The good news was that the winds looked favorable, so far. I had also gotten a look at a CNN weather picture the day before, so I knew that no major weather systems were forecast to hit Louisiana that day. I decided to go for it. I had survived the undercover mission to this point. It would not be right to have to ditch in the ocean after all I had been through already, so it just wouldn't happen. Mind over matter. I would will it to be so.

Since I could transmit over the radio, I called the New Orleans Air Branch over a special long-range radio every hour. I told them about my predicament. I didn't know if they heard me or not, but if they did, I had a plan.

There was an intersection of two airways about a hundred miles south of New Orleans. I radioed that I would be at that intersection at a certain time. I kept broadcasting this message every hour as I flew across the Gulf. At precisely the time that I crossed the intersection, a customs Citation pulled up beside my wing.

I radioed for them to rock their wings if they heard me. They did. I then told them to lead the way back to Belle Chasse, and I would fly off their wing as a flight of two. From that point, they handled all the radio reports needed for me to enter the country and land. I landed with thirty minutes of fuel remaining, safe and sound—but the day wasn't over yet!

I still had a meeting with the man from Atlanta in two hours at the Slidell Airport. He still believed that I was flying there direct from Belize with the marijuana. He had bought an old van and put in a new engine and done a lot of other mechanical work. It still looked like an old van, but it ran perfectly. He told me that it was a lot less likely that he would get stopped by police in an old van. Little did he know.

We had a plan to put some of the NO SHIT team members in the woods near the airport. Other team members, along with some customs special agents, would be ready to come in and arrest him as soon as he met my plane and loaded up the dope.

We had gotten six bales of marijuana from the customs evidence storage facility and put them in the plane. He would never know that I had not picked it up in Belize. I was ready to go as soon as the SRT team got into place. Suddenly, a customs pilot came over to me and asked if I had checked the weather. He said that a line of thunderstorms had popped up and would be in our area in an hour.

I checked the radar. Sure enough, the storms were coming, and if I didn't take off now and do this deal, there was no way I could do it for several hours. We had a line of communication set up with the man from Atlanta. An agent, posing as my friend, would call him and give him updates on my position. He was acting as if he had radio communications with my plane.

We pushed up the transfer, and I jumped into the airplane and headed to Slidell, hoping I could beat the weather. I did mention that nothing is ever simple, didn't I? I didn't realize it at the time, but due to the last minute rush, the arrest team did not have time to get in place.

I landed at the small airport and parked on a section of the ramp far away from other planes and vehicles. A few minutes later, a van pulls up beside me. The man from Atlanta jumps out and opens his back door. I pitch down the bales of grass and he loads them into the van.

The whole thing took less than a minute. He was sweating and very nervous and in a hurry to get out of there. I tried to stall, but to no avail. He drove off in a rush and I was left standing there, wondering where the arrest team was.

I watched him leave the airport and disappear down the roadway. I don't believe that this was in the plan. The only thing I could do was to get back in the airplane and make a radio call. I called on the tactical frequency that every arrest team should be monitoring, "Gentleman, I don't know if can hear me or not, but the dope has left the airport in a green van."

It turned out that another van, loaded with agents, was approaching the airport at just that moment, and they had just passed the green van! Well, of course, they turned around and caught it. Another arrest, another drug dealer off the streets.

I got back in the plane just as the rain began. The clouds were low and the sky turbulent. I was completely drained, physically and mentally. It was only a fifteen-minute flight back to Belle Chasse, but with the bad weather and my mental state, it seemed like an eternity.

I just about kissed the ground myself after I landed. This case was finally over, at least my part. I later got nominated for the Customs Officer of the Year award for my undercover work. I didn't win the award, but it was still a big honor to be one of only five others nominated out of over fifty thousand customs employees. I did get a quality step increase, a kind of federal employee pay increase that bumped me up to a higher pay grade. Nice!

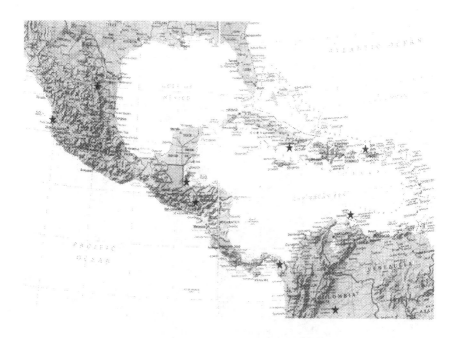

Stars show places of interest mentioned in this book.

President Bush on the day the WWII Memorial was dedicated.

President Clinton in Washington D.C.

Steven Segal preparing for a Blackhawk flight.

Author with Citation

The Citation, CBP's jet interceptor.

AStar helicopter in the Arizona desert looking for UDA's.

Island off of Puerto Rico where the Chinese were abandoned.

The Huey, the first helicopter I flew for U.S. Customs.

The Blackhawk helicopter used by U.S. Customs and Border Protection.

Formation flight over the Superdome in New Orleans.

F-15 flight with General Soileau.

Air Force One in Belle Chasse, La.

$10 million worth of cocaine seized in the Virgin Islands.

The rock island in the US Virgin Islands where we found 880 lbs of cocaine.

Radar site in Puerto Rico

Island off of Belize where I landed during an undercover operation.

Rounding up undocumented aliens in Arizona. The three month
operation netted over 50,000 UDA's.

CBP's Hurricane Ike response in Houston, TX.

Airport at Guantanamo Bay, Cuba.

Arizona Border Control Initiative in Tucson. The largest non-military helicopter operation in United States history.

CBP's fast boat interceptor.

Snowing in south Louisiana the night of the 38,000 lb marijuana bust.

CHAPTER TEN

I guess word got out to all the other customs SAC offices across the country that there was this crazy pilot in New Orleans who would do any undercover mission. I began getting calls to do some really strange cases. When an agent comes up with an idea to set up an undercover operation, the agent must first run it by a supervisor, and the supervisor runs it by his supervisor, etc. The bigger the case, the more levels it has to go through to get approved. If it was going to cost a lot of money or was extremely dangerous, it was usually not approved. Most of the ideas never made the cut. But it did not have to be a crazy plan to be dangerous. One of the closest times I ever came to getting shot was supposedly a simple little undercover case in Atlanta.

It was a money laundering case. We had word from an informant that a big diamond broker in Atlanta was laundering money for the drug cartels. The customs agents based in Atlanta needed a pilot to fly one of the suspects from Atlanta to Panama City, Florida for an undercover meeting. My role was to be a pilot and enforcer for a big drug cartel working out of Colombia. Our cartel needed to exchange a few million dollars for diamonds, off the books of course. We could then sell the diamonds in Europe to someone we knew for cash. It was a way to clean some of the money we had.

To help convince the diamond dealer that we were who we said we were, I flew him down to Panama City. I picked him up at a small airport in Atlanta in the Navajo, the same plane I had flown to Belize. I let him sit in the co-pilot seat, since only he and I were in the plane. I guess he had never flown in a small plane before; as soon as we took off he started turning white. I thought he was going to hurl in my cockpit! I moved him to the back, which was set up for executive seating with a lot more room and comfort. It turned out that he was not air sick. He was just overwhelmed and frightened by the cockpit view as we took off over downtown Atlanta. What a wimp!

We landed in Panama City and took a car that agents had left for us at the airport to the hotel where the meeting was to take place. It was not an ordinary hotel room. The undercover agent, who was posing as the cartel money man, had rented a thousand-dollar-a-day penthouse suite in one of the nicest hotels on the beach.

I escorted the suspect up to the suite and introduced him to the undercover agent. We started discussing our business proposal. To show that we were serious, the agent told me to go down to my room and pick up the money so the suspect could see it. I said okay, and I left the suite.

Now this was all news to me. I didn't even know I had a room! Another agent met me in the hall and took me to a nearby suite that was supposedly mine. It had several large rooms. One had a Jacuzzi with a fantastic view overlooking the beach and Gulf of Mexico. I immediately started trying to figure a way to delay my flight back to Atlanta so I could spend the night here.

I picked up a large duffle bag that the agents had placed in the room and looked inside. It was filled with cash. It was the largest amount of cash I had ever seen. This was the bait money we were going to use to get the diamonds.

Before leaving my room, I watched the live video of the undercover agent and the suspect in the other room. Several agents were sitting around a table also watching this video, ready to come to the rescue if needed. The meeting was also being recorded for court evidence. As I listened, the agent was telling the suspect about me. He was building me up as a cartel enforcer, a very bad guy who would kill you in a second if you crossed him or if he was ordered to by the cartel. My normal way of handling problem people was throwing them out of the airplane over the ocean. This was just great. I'm sure this made the suspect very anxious to ride back to Atlanta with me.

I knew why he was telling the suspect this tale about me. It was for our safety. When we got ready to exchange the money for the diamonds, it was important for him to know that if he tried to rip us off, it would be very bad for him. I hoped that this would keep any funny business from happening. Unfortunately, the story backfired and almost got me killed!

I flashed the cash to the suspect. Just enough of a peek for him to see that we had some serious money. There was only $250,000 in hundred-dollar bills in the bag, but we had it fixed up to look like a lot more. He took the bait, and we set up a time to make the diamond buy, back in his office in Atlanta. It's amazing what some people will do for a large bag filled with hundred-dollar bills.

I flew him back to Atlanta, and, for some reason, he was a little quieter than when we had flown up. He did tell me an interesting story about a friend who had laundered some money in Las Vegas. There was a pit boss at a certain casino there who was in on the laundering scheme. The guy would take the money to a certain high roller gambling room where he was the only person at the table. He'd start betting the money he wanted laundered, usually large sums. It didn't matter what his cards were, in the end he'd win exactly the amount they'd had agreed on. The casino kept 20 percent and he walked away with clean money and receipts that would show that he had won it.

The next day we were all set up to make the deal. We were going to buy $1 million in diamonds. If this deal worked out, we would come back in a week and buy $7 million more. This is what we told him anyway. What was really going to happen was, as soon as we made this first deal, customs agents were going to come in and arrest him and serve a search warrant on his business. We hoped that this would lead us to several organizations that were using the diamond business to launder their money.

The next morning, the customs undercover agent and I were outside the office preparing to go inside. The agents were a little concerned about the $1 million in cash we were carrying. I had a pistol, and they cautioned me to be extremely alert for someone coming into the meeting and trying to steal the cash. The diamond business was located in a high-rise office building in downtown Atlanta, overlooking the football stadium.

A special response team would sneak in and would be hiding one floor below our meeting. They would hit the office as soon as our meeting was over, but there would be a time when we would be alone with the cash. It would be up to me to protect it. I thought to myself, "screw the cash, what about me?" I guess they were more concerned about losing the money than about me. But that's the life of an undercover agent.

Minutes before we walked into the building to make the deal, the deputy United States attorney, who was making some last minute changes to the warrant, just happened to walk by another US attorney's desk and notice that he was also preparing a warrant for the same address. He knew that something was not right and began questioning his colleague.

The attorney told him that an informant had told the DEA that a major drug cartel was going to attempt to launder some money in a diamond exchange business. He was preparing an arrest warrant for the cartel members when they exchanged the cash for the diamonds. A DEA "special response team" was hiding in a back room at the diamond business and would jump out and make the arrest as soon as the exchange was made.

The DEA was excited because these were major cartel members and one of them was a bad-ass enforcer who had probably killed fifty people. The DEA was not going to take any chances and would come out shooting if this guy went for a gun. Are you paying attention? That was me they were talking about!

We were already in the building and walking to the elevator when we got the word to call off the mission. Five minutes later and I would have been making the deal when the door would have burst open and guys would have come in pointing guns at me. I was already on high alert, expecting to be robbed, so I would have had my pistol very close at hand. If, during the confusion, I had reached for my gun, they would have undoubtedly shot me. There's no doubt that I would have gone for my gun with someone bursting in like that. I might have even shot at them. Anyway, it was a very close call. I always thought that it be ironic, after all the dangerous undercover missions I had done, to end up being shot by a fellow law enforcement officer.

If you are a little confused, let me straighten you out. The diamond broker, whom we were going to arrest, had gotten spooked and had gone to the DEA about us. So basically, this turned into what we call a blue-on-blue situation. That is where one law enforcement agency unknowingly goes against another. It's kind of like a friendly fire situation in combat, and it's often a fatal confrontation.

But luckily, this was called off with minutes to spare. All the undercover work once again turned out to be for nothing. I was beginning to wonder if I should just stick to flying.

Not long after the Atlanta case, I was asked to do another undercover mission in Philadelphia. This one was really a very simple one. I was to fly an undercover agent up to Philadelphia to meet with a guy who was selling a large amount of illegal firearms. The agent was posing as a buyer for a drug cartel that needed weapons to protect their poppy fields. I was simply his pilot and bodyguard. How much simpler could the mission be?

It turned out that it was actually a very simple case. I wouldn't even mention it but a couple of things happened that I thought were very funny.

We flew into Philadelphia and had several hours before the undercover meeting, so, along with another customs pilot who had come with me, I decided to check out some of the historical sites. Philadelphia is the home of Independence Hall and the Liberty Bell. Independence Hall, if you recall, is where our founding fathers signed the Declaration of Independence.

The architecture of the Hall was very impressive, especially since it was built in the late 1700s. The Liberty Bell is on display and you can walk right up and touch it. The customs pilot I was with was kind of a jokester, and he started asking the exhibit guard if he knew there was a crack in the bell. Then, he tried to convince the guard to let him fix it with some JB weld. This conversation went on for several minutes, and a crowd was gathering. If you don't find this funny, I guess you would have had to be there.

The meeting location was changed, and we had to fly the undercover agent over to a small airport about a hundred miles away. We had to rush to the airplane and take off so that we could meet the new timetable. In our rush, we did not have time to thoroughly check out the airport where we were asked to land. When we were only a few minutes from landing, I checked the runway length and discovered that it was really short for the size of airplane we were flying.

Of course, being the professional pilots we were, we decided we would land there anyway. Besides, the undercover case was a very big deal, and if we didn't make the meeting on time, it could blow the deal. I landed the King Air with no problem. I had at least one or two hundred feet of runway remaining. The runway was so narrow that I had to reverse the engines and back up the airplane in order to turn around and taxi to the ramp.

When we got out of the airplane and walked inside the small airport terminal building, I noticed several people looking at us. I just figured that they'd never seen a professional pilot who could land in such a short distance. The airport manager soon explained to me why everybody was staring. It turned out that there was a weight limit for aircraft landing at this small airport. Of course, my airplane was far over that limit. Paperwork would be filed with the Federal Aviation Administration, and I could expect a large fine and possibly the suspension of my pilot's license.

I was polite, but basically I told him to do whatever he had to do. I couldn't badge him because I was undercover, remember. Now here's the funny part. The pilot's license I was using had a fake name. The airplane I was flying had a fake registration number. So, when he filed a complaint with the FAA, they would tell him that no such person and no such airplane existed. I am sure he is still scratching his head over that one.

The meeting was uneventful, and we ended up arresting the guy for selling us two hundred illegal AK-47 automatic rifles.

The regional agent in charge came up with a plan to start up an aviation charter business at the Lakefront Airport, located on Lake Pontchartrain, just a few miles from downtown New Orleans. We had heard that there was some smuggling going on out of this airport, so we planned to go undercover, as a dirty airplane charter outfit that was willing to fly anything if the money was right. We hoped that we could draw out the smugglers.

We rented a small office in one of the airplane hangars and set up shop. I had flown air charters in my life before customs, so it was an easy role. I got an expensive undercover car and I had three months to mingle with the local pilot population and develop a case. Another agent worked in the office to help me out.

Every morning, I would drive over to Lakefront and just hang out. I would talk to pilots around the airport as they came and went. It was a long shot that someone would approach me about smuggling for them, and I told the RAC it was probably a waste of time. But he had some seized money from another undercover operation that he needed to spend, so it was worth taking the chance.

After I spent three months pretending to be someone else, we called off the operation. I had met a few shady characters but nothing we could turn into a smuggling case. By now, I was burned out from being undercover and ready to get back to flying full time. I had a lot of fun on all of my undercover adventures, but the customs air program was moving in a new and exciting direction and my time playing secret agent man had finally come to an end. Customs was starting to deploy pilots to the Caribbean and to Central and South America, and they needed all the pilots they could get. I sure wasn't going to miss out on that.

But before I could start flying south of the border, another mission popped up that only I could do. The reason only I could do it was that it involved an old acquaintance of mine who was in prison. This man was a personal friend and chief smuggling pilot for Pablo Escobar, America's number-one most-wanted criminal!

CHAPTER ELEVEN

Pablo Escobar, you may remember, was the head of the Medellin drug cartel in Colombia. At that time, he was responsible for smuggling more illegal drugs into the United States than anyone else. He dealt mostly with cocaine, and he was by far the biggest smuggler on the planet. He was very violent and killed his rivals like they were flies. He had arrest warrants against him in almost every state. The problem was that Colombia would not extradite him to the United States, and he wasn't stupid enough to leave Colombia.

Pablo was the one who got the credit for starting the drug cartels. Before the drug cartels were formed, there were maybe twenty different groups smuggling out of Colombia. Cocaine was just starting to be the new drug of choice in America. The United States all of a sudden was being flooded with coke, and law enforcement was way behind the curve in solving the problem. Airplanes and boats were invading our borders, filled with cocaine to feed the demand. This was the main reason customs started an air interdiction program in the first place—to stop the flow of these drugs.

He quickly grew powerful, and pretty soon we had a ruthless billionaire crazy man, Pablo Escobar, smuggling huge amounts of cocaine into our country. That's where I come in. I had a plan to stop him!

I got into this case by watching an episode of *America's Most Wanted*. The episode was about a man who had been arrested in Puerto Rico for smuggling in a load of cocaine. He was in prison there, and someone broke him out by landing a helicopter in the prison yard.

He was later captured in the United States and was now behind bars at a federal prison in Atlanta. His face looked familiar! I seemed to have heard the name before. I began researching the case and found out that he used to fly from the same small airport where I had learned to fly. After I thought about it, I remembered that there had been some strange flight activities going on at that airport while I was learning to fly. Of course, back then I wasn't the highly trained investigator I was now.

After discovering that I had met this man before, I went to speak with the regional agent in charge in the Office of Investigations and my branch chief. I requested permission to go interview this man. If I could get him to talk, he would undoubtedly have a lot of useful information pertaining to air smuggling. They quickly agreed, and I was off to Atlanta.

The prison in Atlanta was surrounded by a huge gray wall, similar to that of a medieval castle. As I entered, my mind flashed back to another prison I had been in. My senior year at college, I had worked at the Tennessee State Prison in Nashville. While attending Middle Tennessee State University during the day, I worked the 11 p.m. to 7 a.m. shift at the prison. And on top of that, I drove eighty miles a day, back and forth between school and work. No, I didn't walk three miles through the snow, all uphill, to school every day as my grandfather always claimed he did, but that would have been easier.

While we're talking about the Tennessee State Prison, I may as well tell you that story. I was almost shot there, too. It was back in the seventies, and prisons were not as kind and gentle as they are today. There was a rule that a prisoner could not raise his hands above his waist while being escorted in the prison yard. If he did, he could be shot by a tower guard. Towers were spaced every hundred feet or so around the prison wall. Each was manned with an armed guard.

One night, about two in the morning, I picked a prisoner up in his cell block and was escorting him to the medical department to get his medication. It was a clear, cold night, and it was just him and me walking across this huge open yard in the middle of the prison. Suddenly, a huge meteor passed overhead, and he instinctively pointed up at it. Little did I know that a tower guard was watching us and saw the prisoner raise his hands.

An hour later, I was in the chow hall getting a snack, and this tower guard walks over to me. He said he had seen the prisoner raise his hand in the yard and had aimed his rifle to take a shot, but the prisoner had lowered his hand, so he didn't shoot. I looked at this guard. He was an old man who wore thick glasses. It was very dark out in the yard, and the rifle he had aimed at the prisoner was a lever action Winchester. If you know your guns, yes, that's the same gun you see in cowboy movies. It had to be eighty years old.

I had to qualify with one at the range, because I also had tower guard duty. The sights were so bad on these old rifles that you were lucky to hit the side of a barn. The thought of this old guard taking a hundred-yard shot, at night, with me standing one foot away from this prisoner sent chills down my spine. I just smiled at him. What could I say? I'm pretty sure this guy remembered back to the time when this rifle was new. I wasn't sure just who were the scariest people in that prison—the prisoners or the guards.

The prison was so overcrowded that they had to use the gym as a cell block. Bars had been set up over about half of the basketball court, which made it look like a big bird cage. They put more than two hundred prisoners in there. One night, I was guarding this block and heard some screaming from inside. It was nighttime, and most of the lights were out. Most of the prisoners had put up blankets around their bunk beds for privacy, so it was sort of a maze in there.

At night, since the prisoners were sleeping, only one guard was assigned to this area, and it was against policy to open the cell door unless you turned on all the lights and called in five other guards for help. One of the prisoners came to the door all bloody, asking for help. Other prisoners were trying to kill him.

Now, being the only guard there at the time, I couldn't just open the door. If this guy was faking, I could be overwhelmed by a rush of prisoners. I called for some help and got him out of there as quickly as possible. While I had the extra backup, I took a walk through the cell block. It was spooky, like walking through a pit filled with rattlesnakes.

I often was assigned to work on death row. Since I was on the midnight shift, everyone was usually asleep. So I would sit in the electric chair, "Old Sparky," and read a book. For someone never convicted of a crime, I had spent a lot of time in prison. Anyway, as I walked into the Atlanta prison all these things ran through my mind.

I met with the prisoner in a small room along with another customs special agent. There was only a fifty-fifty chance he would even talk to me. He was looking at thirty years in prison, so why should he? I introduced myself as a pilot. That got his interest right away. He was a pilot, and pilots connect on a certain level that non-pilots don't understand. It's kind of an unspoken word that yes, I too have broken the earthly boundaries and have soared through the skies.

When he found out that I had learned to fly in his hometown and knew a lot of the same people that he knew, it was like we were old friends in five minutes. He had never talked to any law enforcement officers before, especially ones who knew what questions to ask. He turned out to be a treasure trove of important information.

He was Escobar's main pilot, had flown over thirty loads of drugs himself, and had also trained many others to fly them. He was like the brains behind the air smuggling part of Escobar's operation. Pablo liked him so much that he had paid $500,000 for the helicopter prison break in Puerto Rico. He gave us a great deal of information that helped us understand how the cartel operated. We discovered that Escobar was even smuggling into Africa and Spain. The special agent wrote all this information into a report that went to every customs office in the country.

But as helpful as this information was, it was not what I had come for. I wanted to capture Escobar and I needed this guy's help to do it! We discussed several ways to make a capture possible and finally arrived at what I figured to be the best plan.

He was certain that he could get Pablo on the phone. Few people could do this. There was a large-scale manhunt underway during this time, and all the king's horses and all the king's men had not even gotten close to finding Escobar. If we could get him on the phone, we had ways to track the phone's location. If we had special response teams standing by in different parts of Colombia, we could swoop down on his location and arrest him. It would be a big operation, but one likely to succeed. Even Colombia was after Escobar at that time, so I was thinking we could also get their help, or at least their permission.

I flew back to my office and had a meeting with the RAC and the branch chief. This was going to be a major international event, so naturally we had to channel this through headquarters in Washington, D.C. I had experienced in the past that taking a plan to that level usually meant the end of it. With too many politicians and lawyers looking at it and too much worrying about what would happen if things went wrong, it would never be approved. Even if headquarters loved the plan, it would suddenly be *their* plan. But I never cared who got credit for any of my cases. I just wanted to catch bad guys.

Much to my surprise, a few days later I got word that someone from Washington was coming down to meet with me. This turned out to be one of the top men in DEA. He was *the* man in charge of America's effort to capture Escobar.

He wanted to know my entire plan in minute detail. After I had laid out my plan, he said that he liked it a lot and that we might put it into play in a couple of weeks, if needed. He said that, before we went to all the trouble of getting this expensive plan set up, I needed to know that they were already close to capturing Escobar. In fact, they had missed him by only minutes that very morning. The breakfast on the table where he was hiding out, was still warm when the authorities had arrived.

He also told me that when they did find Escobar, he didn't think he would be captured alive. I knew the reason for this. Escobar had been arrested by the Colombians already and was put in a special prison—where he had continued conducting business as usual. When Escobar had gotten tired of pretending to be in prison, he simply escaped. That was the reason for the big manhunt. Nobody wanted a repeat of that prison fiasco.

The DEA man left to go back to D.C. I received no further word from him. But a week later, I was watching CNN news, and got all the word I needed: Pablo Escobar had been killed by a sniper from a special response team that had tracked him down while he was talking on a cell phone. Soon after, the prisoner who was helping me in Atlanta was transferred to the top maximum security prison in the country. Now, I'm sure that all of this happening just a few days after I had discussed this exact scenario was just a coincidence … if you believe in coincidences. I was just glad we had eliminated one of the world's leading criminals.

I had gotten another important bit of information from this prisoner that is worth mentioning. To help in the air war on drugs, the US Air Force was flying AWAC airplanes in the Gulf of Mexico and places further south. An AWAC is a large, four engine, airliner-sized jet with what looks like a huge pie plate on top. Its sophisticated radar can pick up any airplane within a two-hundred-mile radius around it. Since there was very little radar south of our border, the AWACs played a very important role in stopping airplane smuggling. If they found a target , they would call customs aircraft in to intercept and follow it.

Almost as soon as the AWACs were deployed, the air targets dropped off quickly. No one could figure out why they were not picking up any illegal targets. They moved the AWACs around to different locations, but still no targets. Their schedules were classified, so few had access to them. Of course customs did, as well as a few other key military sites south of the border.

I now had information from the prisoner that a colonel in the army was selling the AWACs schedules. I even had his name. He was working at a Honduran military compound, which was sort of their equivalent to our Pentagon.

This was big! Once again, I found myself in a case of national importance, I'm not sure how I kept getting myself involved in things like this, but it was exciting.

I soon met with an air force investigative group that was also interested. I even had to go to the Pentagon and brief army CID (Central Investigative Division). They are the army equivalent to the navy NCIS, like on the TV show.

Once we identified and verified that the colonel in question had been assigned to Honduras during the correct time period, I thought we had our man. He was stationed in Ft. Benning, Georgia and working at the School of the Americas. This school was under fire from the press and Congress for training and equipping soldiers for Central and South America countries. Some of these soldiers had left their military units and were working for the drug cartels as mercenaries.

With all that was going on at this special school, I now had to go and talk to the school commander, a full bird colonel. I was sure that the last thing he needed was to hear that someone under his command was selling secrets to the enemy. It could be the last nail in the coffin for the school.

He was in an "I can't believe this is happening to me mood," but he ordered in the suspect colonel. Believe it or not, it was the wrong colonel! After interviewing him and checking out his stories, I found out that there was an army colonel from the Honduran army by the exact same name, who had been stationed there at the exact same time. It was a relief for me that one of our own was not a traitor. It was probably a big relief for him, too. We turned the information over to the Honduran authorities and I never heard another word about it.

CHAPTER TWELVE

During the time I was doing undercover and investigative work, I was still flying a great deal. After all, I was hired to be a pilot. I had needed considerable training to learn to fly all the different sophisticated and complex aircraft I flew. In the early years of my career, it seemed that all I did was go from one school to the next. I once started counting all the schools and training classes I had attended—I stopped counting at seventy-five. Some of these were one or two days long, and some lasted several months.

Customs pilots were probably the best trained pilots in the world at what we did, which was air interdiction. We had pilots from every branch of the military service, as well as former airline, charter, and instructor pilots. Someone in the group had flown just about every aircraft there was to fly. We took the best of all these experiences and shaped them into our own standard operating procedures.

When I was hired, I was already an experienced helicopter pilot, but to fly the Blackhawk, a military helicopter, I had to attend the Army UH-60 Blackhawk Aircraft Qualification Course in Ft. Rucker, Alabama.

Ft. Rucker is an army base, and it had the largest helicopter flight school in the world. I had to spend seven lovely weeks there learning to fly the "army way." I was the only non-army guy in my class. (My two-year army career in the 70s had included no flying.) The actual flying we did at Ft. Rucker was really very good training. We did NVG (night vision goggles) and sling loading, where you lift five-thousand- pound weights attached to a cable under the helicopter. I had never done any of this type flying before, and I enjoyed it.

On the civilian helicopters we had, like the Jet Ranger and the AStar, customs contracted out the training to civilian flight schools. During the last ten years of my career, I primarily flew the AS-350 B2 AStar helicopter. A company in Orange County, California had our training contract, and I really enjoyed going there and flying for three days every year.

On one of the days we did our mountain training we would fly up into the San Bernardino Mountains, just north of Los Angeles. We would fly around these majestic mountains, landing on rocks and mountain tops and confined spaces in the trees.

We would end the day by landing on Mt. Baldy, which was a little over ten thousand feet in elevation. The views from these mountains were fantastic, and on a clear day you could see the entire L.A. valley.

Going and coming from the mountains to Orange County, we would fly over the Hollywood sign and some of the movie stars' homes in Beverly Hills. Of course, strictly for the training value, we would make a low pass over the Playboy Mansion and also down the beaches where they filmed Baywatch. It was all great training, but mostly, it was great fun.

My job was not all training. On a typical day back at the Air Branch office, I would do a radar patrol in the Gulf of Mexico if I was assigned a Citation, and a bayou patrol if I was assigned a helicopter. If we found a suspicious airplane or boat, we would follow it until we could determine who it was and what it was up to.

Of course, other missions would pop up all the time. One day, I was flying the Blackhawk around the Chandelier Islands, just south of Biloxi, looking for marijuana that had been washing up on the beaches. I got a call that officers needed assistance in an area near Moss Point, Mississippi. When you get calls like that you respond immediately. Lives could be on the line.

I learned more about what was happening on my way there. A Mississippi highway patrolman had pulled over a car for speeding. Somehow, a fight had ensued, and the speeder had managed to get the officer's pistol. The guy had shot the patrolman and run into some nearby woods with the weapon. Now he was armed and obviously dangerous, so anything could happen. This was all taking place on Interstate 10, a very busy roadway. The highway patrol officers needed a helicopter to help find the suspect.

When I arrived at the scene, there had to be ten police cars there. They had completely blocked I-10 to allow me to land and pick up some local officers who were familiar with the area. I landed on the interstate, amused at the traffic that was backed up for miles. Sometimes it was fun to be in law enforcement. Who else could get by with things like this? And things like this happened all the time.

I often had to land on highways, sometimes in the middle of the city. I did many surveillances where I would fly at a low level through the high-rise buildings of a major metropolitan area. We did what had to be done to protect life and property.

After we had searched for an hour, the speeder gave himself up. I have witnessed this on many such occasions. When people see that a helicopter is looking for them they almost all come to the conclusion that it is useless to run. Resistance is futile.

I remember a search in Alabama. I was helping look for an escaped prisoner. We had searched for hours in a wooded area, but he was not to be found. This guy had obviously not gotten the message about giving up if a helicopter was after you. Maybe he had some mental problems. I was getting tired of flying. The trees were thick, and I had to hover low to see into them. Helicopters are subject to certain aerodynamic restrictions, called a height-velocity diagram. Pilots called it the dead man's curve. What it means is that you have to have a certain amount of altitude or a certain amount of airspeed to be able to safely land if your engine quits working.

It seemed that, in law enforcement, we often had to fly in this dead man's curve to be able to accomplish our mission. We straddled a fine line between being safe and getting the mission done. One of our customs pilots, whom I had flown with a week earlier, learned the hard way about flying inside this curve—he was killed out in Arizona.

That tragedy was in my mind while I was flying the Alabama search. Suddenly, I heard a "shots fired" call over the radio. I was hoping that someone had finally found the escapee. It turned out that one of the officers on the ground had killed a rattlesnake that was about to strike him. We later found the escapee at a friend's house. He wasn't even *in* the stupid woods!

I was excited about my Blackhawk mission for the day. President Clinton was coming to visit New Orleans and I was to fly "top cover" with some secret service agents. Air Force One landed at the Belle Chasse Navy Base and parked no more than a nine iron shot away from my office. I had never seen the big 747 up close. With the paint scheme and all, it is really an impressive airplane.

I have stood beside it several times in my career but one time I nearly flew into it! I was flying the Citation out of Houston and we were practicing intercept training. We had a single engine Cessna 210 as the target, and I was in the Citation refining my intercept techniques. We knew that the president was coming to town. We also knew that the FAA had put a twenty-mile no-fly zone around him at all times, even in Air Force One.

Knowing all of this, I had planned my mission on the northwest side of Houston, some fifty miles from where the president was supposed to be. We were all busy doing the intercepts when we noticed an aircraft in our flight path. It turned out to be Air Force One, descending into Houston. The president's pilots often took roundabout routes from point A to point B to confuse anyone on the ground with evil intentions.

The plane passed close enough that I could read United States of America on the side. Of course, this was not my fault, so it was all good. I never heard anything about it. I did almost have a collision with another high profile airplane, and on that occasion, you might say it would have been my fault!

This was before my customs job. I was flying a Piper Cheyenne airplane out of Memphis, Tennessee to a little town about ninety miles to the north. I was alone in the cockpit, and it was a clear day so I wasn't on a flight plan. It was just a short little hop that did not require me to talk with a ground radar controller over most of the trip. I had just leveled off at fifty-five hundred feet when I saw a movement out of my peripheral vision. It was low and in a formation, and I thought at first that it was a flock of geese.

Whatever it was, it was moving very fast and coming under me. Suddenly, I realized that it was the Blue Angels! Then I remembered they were doing an air show at the Arlington Navy Base, which I was now flying over. But wait, that was not until tomorrow. Could this be a practice day? Shouldn't Memphis Approach Control have warned me about this? It didn't matter now.

The flight of five F-18 fighter jets turned straight up in perfect formation and headed right for me. It was all happening so quickly that I didn't know which way to turn. The formation went from ground level to my flight level in seconds. They passed so close that I could see the sunglasses on the pilot's faces. They never broke formation. I have always wondered if they even saw me that day, the day I almost made history as being the one who took out the entire Blue Angels demonstration team.

That's the way things happen in aviation. One second you are flying along minding your own business—and the next second you are in extreme danger. Most of the time, the problem is another aircraft that is trying to share the airspace with you. Sometimes it is a large bird that zooms by your windshield, missing by only inches. Before your heart can even skip a beat, the danger has usually come and gone. I had many close calls that could have gone either way. Too many to think about, in fact, so let's move on.

Getting back to flying security for Clinton in New Orleans. That was the only time I had ever heard air traffic controllers tell me, "Do whatever you want. The airspace is yours." They had grounded all aircraft in New Orleans except for mine. This was sometimes a pretty cool job!

Helicopter missions were not the only ones that popped up. One day, we got a call from a special agent who needed help in the Cayman Islands. This tiny group of islands is located south of Cuba in the Caribbean Sea. The agents had completed an undercover boat mission involving intercepting a load of heroin from Colombia. They had eight hundred pounds of it and were afraid the bad guys would regroup and attempt to get the dope back. They felt that their lives could be in danger, so they needed to get the heroin and themselves out of harm's way ASAP. I don't know why they were so worried; the dope wasn't worth much more than ten million dollars.

I jumped into the King Air with another pilot, and we were on our way to the Caymans. It was a long flight, but if the winds were in our favor we could make it nonstop from New Orleans. When we arrived in the islands, the agents were anxious to leave as soon as we refueled the airplane. They had received word that the smugglers were about to make a move to get the dope back. They had little backup they could trust, and sitting on all that dope was a little nerve-racking.

We loaded up and started up. Two red lights lit up on the cockpit instrument panel. This indicated a serious problem with the airplane. By that time, all the local law enforcement support that we did have had already left the airport. So here we were, stuck on the ramp with all this dope and with a broken plane. For all we knew, the smugglers were closing in at any minute.

Now, the last thing you really want to do as a pilot is take off with a known problem and fly over a thousand miles of ocean. On the other hand, we didn't really want to be caught in a gun battle with a bunch of pissed-off smugglers, stuck in a foreign country with no backup.

I had never experienced a double bleed air failure before, and I would have bet money that it was a grounding item. I grabbed the maintenance book that we keep in the airplane and turned to the minimum equipment list. This tells you what equipment can be malfunctioning without preventing you from flying the airplane. Believe it or not, you can fly a King Air with a double bleed air failure (under certain restrictions).

Oh well, I would worry about those restrictions later. Right then, it seemed like the right thing to do was to take off. As soon as we were airborne, I carefully read over the restrictions to see how it would impact the flight. I read that we could not pressurize the airplane. That meant we had to stay low in order to breathe. Staying low also meant that we would burn a lot more fuel. The lower a jet engine flies, the more gas it burns.

I did some calculations. We faced a headwind going back which would cause us to take an hour longer to return to New Orleans than it took to come down. We were burning a lot more fuel at this low attitude. I feared we were not going to make it.

Going back was not an option. I was thinking, "Haven't I been in this situation before?" You know, the Belize trip. I made the decision to continue, and if the winds hadn't improved by mid-way, we would divert into Tampa for fuel. Luckily, once again, the winds went against the forecast. We made it to the airport by the skin of our teeth.

Not long after this, another King Air mission came up. This time I was to fly to Houston, pick up a prisoner, and transport him to a prison in Illinois. I should have known something was different about this trip when I arrived at Houston Air Branch. They told me to stay in the airplane. A tow tractor hooked up to the airplane and towed me inside a hangar. Then they closed the hangar doors.

Suddenly, my airplane was surrounded by agents with automatic rifles. In a dark corner of the hangar, a van's headlights flashed. The van door opened, and I could see the prisoner step out. He was in chains from head to toe. Was Hannibal the Cannibal still alive?

The prisoner was escorted inside the plane and buckled down. Three US marshals would be coming along on the ride. The hangar doors opened, and I was towed outside and ordered to take off quickly. It was all so Hollywood.

When we reached our cruising altitude, I looked back at my human cargo. He looked Hispanic but very ordinary. But how was a criminal supposed to look? I didn't know this man, maybe he wasn't that bad. By the time we had landed and the marshals in Illinois had taken him off the airplane, I had shared a few short conversations with this guy. He seemed okay to me.

After he had gone, the marshals told me who he was. He was a hit man for a Mexican drug cartel and had killed more than fifty people that they knew about. Some estimated that he had killed well over a hundred. Well, you can't judge a book by its cover.

I didn't consider all of the flights as work. I got to fly some really fun trips, too. On one trip, I got to fly the King Air to San Diego to pick up some evidence for a trial in Chicago. The flight from San Diego to Chicago took me over the Rocky Mountain ski resorts in Colorado. I like to ski, and it was cool to see the resorts from the air.

Another trip took me to Edmonton, Alberta, Canada. That flight took me up through the Dakotas and I was able to make a low pass over Mt. Rushmore and see the presidents' faces carved in the stone mountain. Edmonton is just about a hundred miles from the Arctic Circle. That's so far north that, since it was summer, it didn't get dark until 11 p.m. Edmonton has a huge shopping mall that has a full-scale replica of the Santa Maria, the ship that Christopher Columbus sailed on to cross the ocean blue, in 1492.

On another trip, also to Canada, I flew a plane back to New Orleans from St. John's, Newfoundland. The weather in St. John's was a little different from any I had ever encountered. The fog got very thick there, just like in New Orleans, but with one difference. It would stay foggy even with the wind blowing thirty miles per hour, and it seemed to always be foggy.

I had gone up to test fly a customs King Air that a company there had modified. After waiting several days for the fog to lift, the company talked me into flying the test flight anyway. They were accustomed to flying in this fog, and, anyhow, after the pilot took off and headed east, he was over ocean all the way to England. In fact, I noticed a sign in town which said that St. John's was closer to London than it was to New York.

Well, they knew the area, so against my better judgment, I agreed, and we departed. At first I could see the ocean below me. It was hard to miss. It was only a few hundred feet below. The worse the fog got, the lower we flew. We had to stay low so that the team could calibrate the marine radar they had installed. Suddenly, a large ship appeared before me. It really wasn't that close, but I got to wondering, "How tall are these ships, anyway?"

Then I started seeing some strange birds soaring past me. They looked like little penguins. I saw some of them dive into the water. The crew explained that they were puffins, a bird that could fly but could also dive down to fifty feet underwater and catch a fish. They had to be twenty pounds each and would easily penetrate the windshield if one hit us. That was enough flying for me, so I climbed up above the fog and headed back to the airport.

On the flight back to New Orleans, I had to refuel in Buffalo, New York. Coincidentally, that was only about five miles from Niagara Falls, so I made a low pass over the Falls. Some people pay good money for sights like that.

We were also still intercepting some airplanes. One intercept that comes to mind demonstrates how effectively customs could chase down and arrest a smuggler flying drugs into the United States. Ground radar controllers had picked up a target crossing over the border from Mexico in the area around Brownsville, Texas. A Citation, launched out of Houston Air Branch, had intercepted the unidentified airplane and was now following it. The Citation was going to need to refuel in Arkansas if the airplane continued north. If it had to break off the chase, there was a good chance the suspect airplane would get away.

I immediately launched in another Citation out of New Orleans. I caught up to the chase in Hot Springs, Arkansas just as the Houston Citation had to break off for fuel. Now, normally the Houston Citation would refuel and leapfrog several hundred miles in front of the chase to be in position to relieve me if I needed to refuel. On this particular occasion, that was not necessary because of the type of airplane we were following. This plane had already flown from Mexico. We calculated that it could not possibly have much more fuel, even with the extra fuel tanks that smugglers often put on their planes.

We notified customs agents on the ground of our progress. They were alerted all the way to Canada that we might need their help. We could also call local police and sheriff's departments if needed. When the airplane started descending, we would alert the appropriate people. If no one was available to help—for instance, if it landed suddenly at a small airport before help could arrive—we were perfectly able to handle the takedown with our Citation crew. If the chase had been closer to the border, a Blackhawk filled with pilots and agents would also be in trail behind us. But this airplane was too fast and too far north of the border for our helicopters to help.

Never underestimate how much fuel a smuggler can put aboard his airplane! This plane did not start a descent until we'd almost reached Chicago! By then, it was dark. It looked like he was landing at a small airport about forty miles south of Chicago. Since customs agents on the ground had been following this chase on the radio for hours, they were in a good position to assist.

I landed behind the airplane and taxied up close behind it. After hours of chasing it all the way from Mexico, the pilot still didn't know we were anywhere around. The plane pulled up to a secluded spot and stopped. We jumped out and were waiting when the pilot opened his door. Man, was he surprised! He had over a thousand pounds of marijuana in the plane.

I could see the blue lights of several agents and police cars in the distance. It turned out that there was a truck waiting to offload the drugs at the airport, and when the customs agents arrived, the driver took off at a high rate of speed. The agents caught him, of course, and within a week, the agents had arrested several others in the Chicago area and had broken up a big smuggling ring.

But not all of my chases went so smoothly. I was chasing another plane one night that was heading into a small airport in a suburb of Memphis. I knew the special agents based in Memphis, so I radioed ahead for them to head for this airport. I told them to just stay back, out of sight, and we would land behind the airplane and effect the arrest. If the smugglers had any accomplices at the airport, we would the special agents' help to chase them down, since we didn't have a vehicle.

The suspect landed, and I was on final approach to land behind it when a car pulled out on the runway in front of me with blue lights flashing. The suspect airplane hadn't even turned off the runway before my overzealous special agent friends were trying to get it to stop. The pilot saw the agent's car behind it and simply took back off. Unfortunately, I was almost out of fuel and could not chase the plane again until I landed and refueled. We followed it until we were certain which direction it was headed, and then we broke off the chase and landed for fuel.

We figured that the suspect must also be low on fuel, so we requested local police assistance to watch all the surrounding airports. We had figured correctly, and by the time I had refueled and was back in the air, the plane had been spotted on the ground at an airport not fifty miles away. The airplane was there but the pilot was not.

I reached the airport within minutes. It was night, and the local police had secured the airplane but had no idea where to start looking for the pilot in the dark woods. I made a few circles around the airport, searching for the pilot with the infrared camera. It didn't take ten minutes to find him hiding behind a tree. He had no idea we could see him in the pitch black night.

We found him—and several bales of cocaine he had hidden in the woods. We also found some boots in the mud beside the airplane.

The pilot had started running away so fast when he saw the police car coming that he had run out of his boots!

This is how the US Customs Service's air interdiction program worked. We did this over and over again, and finally the smugglers started to get the message that air smuggling into America was a losing proposition. They changed tactics, and so did we. We started deploying offshore, to countries like Puerto Rico and Colombia. Soon we were deploying to half a dozen other countries in the Caribbean and in Central and South America. Little did I know that my real adventures were just beginning!

CHAPTER THIRTEEN

Since Puerto Rico is considered a US territory, if a smuggler could get the drugs into that country, the smuggler was home free. There were no US Customs checks between Puerto Rico and the United States. Once the smugglers realized this, they started smuggling drugs through Puerto Rico instead of taking a chance on going directly into the United States. Puerto Rico was also within the fuel range of a typical airplane used by the smugglers flying out of Colombia.

Most of the time they would airdrop to boats a few miles offshore and then return to Colombia. By doing this, they never had to land outside Colombia; therefore, their risk of being arrested was small. Human smugglers also frequently used Puerto Rico. We had quite a Haitian problem at one time, as thousands tried to leave that country and sneak into America. It was a lot easier for them to reach Puerto Rico, which was only a day's boat ride, than to reach America. They knew if they made it into Puerto Rico they stood a good chance of reaching the United States.

The US Customs Service quickly realized that they needed an Air Branch in Puerto Rico. An Air Branch was placed there, but it would take a few years to hire and train all the pilots they needed. So, customs would send down airplanes and flight crews from around the country to help the branch. I was sent down on several thirty-day assignments, flying both the Citation and the Blackhawk. I would see more action there in a month than I would see in a year in New Orleans. But chasing bad guys was only half the fun there. Flying around the islands of the Caribbean was unbelievably beautiful. Imagine having your own helicopter to tour places like the Virgin Islands.

On my first trip to Puerto Rico, I was assigned to fly the Blackhawk helicopter. I thought I was lucky because my co-pilot was very familiar with the area. He had flown charter flights out of San Juan years earlier, so he knew all the surrounding islands very well. On one of our first flights, we decided to get familiar with our area of operations. We took off and flew, very low, down the entire northern coastline of Puerto Rico. We continued on eastbound and flew a loop around the Virgin Islands.

The Virgin Islands were divided into the US Virgin Islands and the British Virgin Islands. On our aviation chart, these islands were all controlled by a San Juan controller. Normally, you need permission to fly a government aircraft inside the territory of another country, but the way that the islands were depicted on the chart, it seemed they were all under US control. I asked my co-pilot, who knew the islands, if we could fly into the British Virgin Islands airspace. He assured me that it was okay, and he said that he used to do it all the time.

My co-pilot loved sailboats. He owned his own sailboat, which he sailed in Lake Pontchartrain, a large lake just north of New Orleans. As we flew along, we would circle any yachts that looked interesting to him. When we were flying along the coastline of the British Virgin Islands, we saw a huge yacht anchored just offshore. Naturally, he had to see it up close. We flew over and circled around it to check it out and then proceeded on with our patrol. It was really a very nice yacht.

Less than ten minutes later, we got a call over the radio to return to base immediately. We did not know what to think. Maybe something good had popped up and they needed us for a different mission.

When we landed back at the branch, we were told to go to the branch chief's office. Now, that is never a good thing. We walked into his office. He was visibly upset. It turns out that the yacht we had circled belonged to the Queen of England. Her mother, the Queen Mother, was onboard. The British security forces on board the yacht had seen this military helicopter heading straight for them, and they had pulled out a surface-to-air missile. Fortunately, they had used a little restraint and had decided not to shoot. This time I was almost killed by the British! My unusual brushes with death continued.

The chief reminded us that we had to have permission to fly in airspace that belonged to another country. Since this was our first day working in this area, he let this be a lesson to us. He even took some of the blame for not having a local pilot flying with us who was familiar with the area.

After we had departed the branch chief's office, I turned to my co-pilot and asked him why he told me it was okay to fly in British airspace. He said he didn't understand, that when he flew helicopter charters he flew over there all the time without any problems. Then it dawned on us that this flight was different—we were in a government aircraft!

A few days later, we were flying over a tiny little uninhabited island about seven miles off Puerto Rico that was often used by human smugglers. As soon as we approached the island, we saw people running into the woods. This time we had a local border patrol agent flying with us. For some reason the branch chief didn't want us flying alone.

This island was basically only a mountain sticking out of the ocean. It had steep cliffs around most of it, but on one side it had a flat area where someone had built a helipad. Next to the helipad was a little harbor where a fishing boat could safely anchor out of the surf.

There was barely room as I landed the huge Blackhawk helicopter on this tiny helipad. I shut down the engines, and the three of us set off on foot to find the people. Whoever they were, they were stranded. There was no way off this island except by boat or helicopter. There were no boats anywhere around.

The island was only about a total of fifty acres, but the woods were thick and there were large hundred-foot foot drop-offs everywhere. This was getting to be dangerous. Finally, we found the five people and led them back to the Blackhawk. They were all Chinese. They were also in bad shape. They had been left on the island two days earlier with no water or food, and they were severely dehydrated.

They had been told by the smuggler, whom they had paid to get them into Puerto Rico, that this island was Puerto Rico! All they had to do was walk over the mountain and there was a town. If we hadn't come along they would have been dead by morning.

We gave them some water, loaded them up, and flew them back to Puerto Rico. We had an ambulance waiting when we arrived. They all survived. After they recovered, we had an interpreter interview them for the full story. They had paid $100,000 each to get into the United States. They had been put in the hull of a ship in China and had not seen the sun for thirty days.

Then, they were transferred to a small boat and dropped off at this island and told it was Puerto Rico. These poor souls had been left to die on an island where they would never be found, unless of course some Tennessee boy happened to fly by in a helicopter. What are the odds?

A few days later, I got a phone call at daybreak and was told to get to the office as soon as possible. When I arrived at the office, I was briefed on the situation. During the night a boat had been spotted by a customs boat patrol, heading for a small island just south of St. Thomas, in the Virgin Islands. This island was no more than a big group of rocks and was less than one mile in circumference.

Smugglers often used it to drop off drugs from boats coming up from Colombia. Later, smaller fishing boats from one of the Virgin Islands would come out and pick up the drugs. It was suspected that the boat that had been spotted during the night had stashed a large amount of drugs on the island.

We needed to get a Blackhawk out to the island for a search before another boat came along and picked up the dope. We blasted off for the Virgin Islands, and I was hoping that this trip would go a little smoother than my last trip.

This tiny island looked like a big pile of rocks from the air. If you look at a map of the Caribbean Sea, you'll notice that there are hundreds of islands. The map only shows about half of them. The whole area is filled with tiny, uncharted islands.

I flew down to about fifty feet off the ground, and we began to slowly search the island. In the back of the helicopter was a Puerto Rican customs pilot, who was very familiar with this island. He said he had found drugs on the island many times. I guess he had an eye for what to look for, because he found several large bales piled in the rocks. The bales were the same color as the rocks and were very difficult to see.

There were so many steep rocks sticking up on this island that there was no place to land the helicopter. We called for a customs boat to come and pick up the dope. We needed to get someone out of the helicopter to help lower the bales from their location in the rocks down to the boat. This turned out to be easier said than done.

I hovered over a towering rock, allowing one of the wheels of the Blackhawk to touch the rock. The two pilots who were riding in the back jumped out. Then, I eased away from the rock so that the blast from the rotor blades would not blow them off the rock and into the ocean, a hundred feet below. Later they told me it was one of the scariest things they had ever done. They were on the pinnacle of this huge rock with hundred-foot drop off on every side and had to climb down to another rock where the bales were located.

The customs boat arrived and the agents helped lower the bales of drugs down to them. Then the pilots got on the boat. There was no way they could get back on the helicopter. We all headed back to St. Thomas, only about thirty miles away. I arrived at the island ahead of the boat and met it at the dock. When we opened up the bales, we found 820 kilos of cocaine, worth millions on the street.

It was going to be a good day, and it still was not even 8:00 a.m. Since we were on the ground in St. Thomas, we decided that it wouldn't be right if we did not take this opportunity to check out the city. St. Thomas, the capital of the Virgin Islands, is definitely one of the most beautiful places in the world. In fact, a small beach a few miles away called Megan's Beach, is considered one the world's most beautiful beaches.

Out about sixty miles on the west side of Puerto Rico is a unique island called Mona Island. It sticks up out of the water like a big flat table. It's about ten miles around, uninhabited, with only limited vegetation. There is a steep cliff surrounding the island, except for one small section on the southwest side. I was told by one of the local pilots that there are caves running throughout the island. Inside one cave is a carving in a rock of a Spanish cross with 1682 carved beneath it.

On the northeast tip of the island is an old, abandoned house with a caved-in roof. Next to the house is a water well with an old-fashioned pump handle. This well is the only source of fresh water on the island. This island was often a stopover point for Haitian illegal immigrants trying to sneak into Puerto Rico.

On our patrols, we often checked out Mona Island for these illegal immigrants. I would come in low when approaching the island so that I could surprise anyone there and not allow them time to hide. One day, I came in, flying a few feet above the wave tops, and I pulled up just before reaching the steep cliffs of the island. I popped up, seemingly out of nowhere, right over this abandoned house. We knew that if there was anyone on the island they would be close to the only water source.

Sure enough, there was this big Haitian standing next to the water pump. He was so shocked I could see the whites of his big eyes a mile away. He was also buck naked! I think he was taking a bath. Within seconds he started to run.

Now, when you think about it, you have to wonder how he thought he was going to get away from a helicopter on an island. But I guess instinct took over, and from my vantage point it was all ass and elbows. Small thorn bushes thickly covered the area where he was running. This guy was very black and soon I could see his legs turning red from blood as the thorns did their work. I hovered around in front of him and kind of sand blasted him with the rotor downwash to discourage him from running. He just changed directions.

I bet we chased this big naked Haitian for ten minutes with no signs of him stopping. Finally, I dropped off one of the Spanish-speaking agents from the back of the helicopter about fifty yards in front of the runner. Then I climbed up a few hundred feet so the two could hear each other over the helicopter noise.

The agent convinced him to surrender. I picked them up and we flew back to the branch and turned him over to the border patrol. I had heard of illegal immigrants arriving in Puerto Rico with just the clothes on their back. This guy arrived with not even that!

That portion of the oceans around Mona Island is called Mona Pass. This was the route the Haitians used to go between Haiti and Puerto Rico. Sometimes they would come through these waters on small boats so overloaded with people that the boats would sink. If the boats didn't sink, often some of the passengers would fall off into the water. It happened so often that the sharks quickly learned that this was a good hunting area.

Mona Pass was filled with sharks. I could see them as I flew over. The sound of the rotor blades striking the ocean created a vibration that caused the sharks to come to the surface. I would fly low just to watch them. One of the agents riding in the back was very afraid of sharks, so we would get a big laugh flying over them and watching his reaction.

One day, we got word that a Coast Guard cutter had spotted a boat full of Haitians coming through Mona Pass. When the boat saw the cutter they tried a high-speed turn and capsized, throwing dozens of people into the water. I later watched the video of the aftermath. Scores of hungry sharks had descended on those in the water and had a feast. The water turned red with blood. People were fighting each other to get on top of the overturned boat.

Unfortunately, there was only room for a few and it looked like a grisly version of "king of the hill." When someone would finally get on top, someone else would throw him off. This went on time after time until only a few remained. You could see the sharks grabbing them as they fell off the boat into the ocean. It was a horrible scene. I never flew low-level over Mona Pass again.

There were several airdrops to boats during my first trip to Puerto Rico. I would go out and locate the boat with the drugs and provide guidance and top cover until our customs boats could arrest the occupants. The customs Air Branches had what they called an Ace award. They gave it in recognition of pilots who were involved in five different law enforcement actions. This copied the air force policy, which recognized a pilot as an Ace if he or she shot down five aircraft during combat.

Back in the United States, few pilots were getting their Ace patches because air smuggling had decreased as customs aircraft and manpower had increased. I got an Ace patch on my first thirty-day trip to Puerto Rico. This Ace program only lasted a few years, and by the time it ended, I had two Ace patches.

I made a later trip to Puerto Rico to do flight tests and evaluations on a new airplane we had acquired. We had taken a surplus army C-12 (King Air) and attached a big box that looked like a canoe to the bottom of the fuselage. Inside this box was a marine search radar used to locate boats. This was the same type plane I had flown up in St. John's, Newfoundland.

We had flown in some technical experts, and we were trying to determine the most effective range and altitude to pick up the small boats that the smugglers were using at that time. A full eclipse of the moon one night coincided with a late night flight I was on. If you have looked up into the sky from your backyard on a clear night, you might have been amazed at all the stars. But with all the lights of the city, you're only seeing a fraction of them. If you're on the ground, even away from the city lights, you can still only see a fraction due to all the pollution in the atmosphere.

Now, if you go far out into the ocean where it is pitch black and climb up beyond the contaminated atmosphere and look at the sky, you will not believe how many stars are visible and how bright they are. I have actually had to use a tinted sun screen to protect my eyes from the moon's glare. If you look at the sky with night vision goggles, it is simply unbelievable.

To be out in perfect conditions watching this eclipse was incredible. Now, you might be thinking that I was having way too much fun at government expense. You could be right, but to my way of thinking, if I was willing to risk my life doing all the things I was doing, I could be forgiven for enjoying a few sights here and there.

A funny thing happened on one of my Puerto Rico trips. US Senator Dennis DeConcini came down to Puerto Rico and visited the Air Branch on a fact-finding mission. I flew him on a tour of the island in the Blackhawk. Our tour ended in San Juan, where he caught an airliner back to Washington. The branch chief and several others were in the back of the helicopter and the chief was pointing out areas of interest where we had found loads of dope and illegal immigrants.

They were talking a lot over the intercom system, and it was hard for us pilots in the front to hear the air traffic controller. When we got close to the San Juan airport and were receiving our landing instructions, there was so much talk coming from the back that my co-pilot forgot who was in the back and yelled over the intercom, *"Shut up in the back!"*

It got really quiet. I looked over at him, and he realized that he had just told a US senator to shut up. Well, as you can imagine, he was teased about this at the office for months afterward. About six months later, he quit working for customs to sell real estate. I hope it wasn't because of this one little incident. He assured me it wasn't. Customs soon installed an isolation switch in the cockpit so that the pilots could turn off the conversations in the back.

I flew the Citation on a few trips to Puerto Rico, but it was not as much fun as the Blackhawk. You could see a lot more of the islands in the jet, but I liked to get down in the weeds, so to speak, where the action was. I would chase the drug planes that had airdropped their loads back toward Colombia or Venezuela, but those governments would not let us enter their countries or airspace.

We needed an end game in those countries to effectively stop the smuggling. Eventually, the powers in Washington, D.C. came to that conclusion, and we started deploying to Colombia. And that is when my job *really* got dangerous!

CHAPTER FOURTEEN

When US Customs began southern operations, we used Howard Air Force Base in Panama City, Panama as our base. On arrival in Panama, the flight crews would spend a few days in briefs and then deploy to Colombia, Peru, or Honduras. During a normal thirty-day rotation, a crew might spend one week at each of these different locations. I was deployed to south ops over a dozen times. Each country was different, but our mission was always the same—to stop the drug-smuggling airplanes and boats.

During this time, the war on drugs was a top national priority. Even the military got into the fight. During the heyday of the war on drugs, Howard Air Force Base was crowded with airplanes. It was hard to find a place to park. On one trip I remember seeing seven customs Citations and four customs P-3s on the ramp at one time. The military had more than fifty other aircraft there, including U-2 spy planes, all dedicated to the war on drugs.

A flotilla of US Navy vessels was in the oceans around Colombia. The ships used their radar to help us find air targets as well as maritime targets. Despite the huge buildup of men and equipment, we were estimating that we were only catching 20 percent of the cocaine coming out of Colombia.

On my first trip to Howard Air Force Base, I flew down in a Citation from New Orleans. I stopped at the Cayman Islands for fuel. I was hoping that my trip through the Caymans was a little less eventful than the previous visit. My flight path took me over the entire length of the Panama Canal. I dropped down to a lower altitude so that I could see better. It was cool seeing the Canal, which I had only read about in geography books.

The Panama Canal links the Atlantic Ocean to the Pacific Ocean. Since sea level in these two oceans is over two hundred feet different, a series of locks is used to lower or raise the ships as they pass through the canal. It is pretty interesting to stand beside a lock and watch an eight-hundred-foot ship being lowered thirty feet. On one trip, I rented a boat and fished for peacock bass on the canal. I was catching them as fast as I could put a hook in the water.

On our first night in Panama, the pilots would stay in a hotel downtown. The pilots that we were relieving would leave the next day, and we would then move to apartment-type buildings on Howard AFB. The drive downtown was always interesting. Traffic was a nightmare in Panama City, made worse by the fact that there were no road signs! The Panama invasion to capture Manuel Noriega had taken place a few months before, and the Panamanians had removed all the street signs to confuse the invading US troops. The signs had never been replaced, so it was a crazy place to drive if you didn't know the streets. We stayed in the same hotel that many Americans hid out in during the invasion.

When we were on duty in Panama, we would launch on suspected air targets coming out of Colombia that were picked up by the navy ships or other ground radar. The smugglers were trying to fly their loads not only to Puerto Rico but to Belize, Mexico, the Bahamas, and, of course, the United States. We had to be very careful when we launched on a target because of the great distances involved and the scarcity of places to refuel.

In the early days, we would launch on a target six hundred miles away. We quickly found that this was a waste of time. The target would be long gone before we could catch it. That's when we started placing Citations in Honduras to intercept northbound targets and in Colombia to intercept returning aircraft that had already dropped their loads.

Normally, after I spent a week in Panama, I would be sent to Colombia. We stayed at a Colombian air force base about a hundred miles southeast of Bogotá called Apiay. This was right in the heart of the Revolutionary Armed Forces of Colombia (FARC) country. Colombia was in a civil war; the FARC was the anti-government revolutionary army that attacked the real Colombian military forces regularly, including attacking the air force base where I was staying.

I should have known that the base was unsafe before I even landed there. I was told to spiral down in a tight turn directly over the airport to land. This was because the perimeter was only secure for a three-mile circle. You never knew when the FARC would take a shot at you if you came in low outside that protected area.

The rooms they put us in, if you could call them rooms, were nothing more than ten–foot- by-twenty-foot shipping containers. The door handles looked like the kind used on walk-in deep freezers. One of the pilots with me told me that these were the same units they had used in Vietnam to store bodies. Now, that made me sleep better at night.

I like to get the lay of the land at any new place I visit, so I decided to walk the road that surrounded the airport runway. Every five hundred feet or so, a Colombian military guard was stationed. These soldiers were just kids. They were holding old rifles that looked to be about three times the age of the soldiers. I wondered if any of those old rifles would really shoot.

Every day, I walked the perimeter road. The soldiers would look at me strangely, but they couldn't speak English and I couldn't speak Spanish, so we never communicated. They were as friendly as they could be without talking.

A little side note here. One day, a flock of hundreds of parrots flew over me and landed in the trees beside me. Those colorful birds cost big money back in the States, and I wondered how I could capture a few of them. I never knew they hung out together in such large flocks like that.

Getting back to my story, one night the base was attacked, and I was told that one of the young Colombian soldiers was killed. I was no longer allowed to walk the perimeter. I always wondered which one of my silent buddies was now gone.

We would fly radar patrols at night when it was illegal for other small airplanes to be flying. Any target at night was probably a smuggler. After we had been doing this a few nights, we found out that the place we were patrolling and the area the smugglers were using to load their airplanes was deep in the heart of FARC controlled territory. If we had to make an emergency landing, we could not expect any rescue from the Colombians. Now isn't that nice? We called it flying over Indian country.

Later, a counter-narcotic US contract plane did crash in Colombia. One of the pilots' bodies was found decapitated, and the other pilot was held captive for four years. We were basically on our own, despite customs management's assurances to the contrary. But we knew the risk and were willing to live with it. Those who couldn't handle it, quit. No one was forcing us to do this job.

One night, I was on patrol when I got a call that a US Navy plane was following a plane that they had just witnessed air dropping a load of drugs to a boat south of Puerto Rico. They were just about to enter Colombian airspace, and they needed me to take the handoff. I was in the only US plane allowed in Colombia at the time. Yes, Colombia was starting to cooperate with us, but only so much.

The Colombians launched an A-37 fighter to assist me. The fighter did not have the air-to-air radar capabilities or the infrared night vision camera that the Citation had, so they would fly off of our wing and we would vector them in for the kill. Yes, you heard that right. There was a short period when Colombia was actually shooting down drug planes. They had shot down over a dozen before something happened that ended this policy. But that is another story. You will have to read about my adventures in Peru to learn about that.

It was dark when I intercepted the suspect airplane. I got in close and determined, by using the Citations forward looking infrared radar (FLIR) camera, that it was a twin-engine propeller airplane called an Aero Commander. The Colombian Air Force fighter was about twenty miles behind me as I chased the Commander.

We were having a lot of trouble communicating with the fighter pilot. None of us on the Citation could speak Spanish. English, however, is the universal language of pilots. Supposedly, every control tower in the world has to be able to communicate with a pilot in English.

The fighter pilot could speak some broken English, but he was hard to understand with his accent. Now, this was a recipe for disaster. This was a life or death situation, at least for the smuggler, and we couldn't even talk. Well, what's the worst thing that could happen?

Did you guess right? Yes, the fighter mistook the Citation for the smuggler's airplane and was getting ready to shoot! My run of almost getting killed by friendly's was going strong.

In broken English, I could just make out enough of the conversation to understand the fighter pilot report that he had the target in his sights and he was requesting permission to shoot. He identified the target as a twin engine American business jet! Oh no, Mr. Bill—that was me!

My co-pilot, who was working the radios, began yelling for him to hold his fire, but I wasn't going to take any chances. I started some evasive maneuvers, hoping to lose the fighter. Remember, he had no radar and was flying with only night vision goggles. I managed to lose the fighter just as I had planned, and a minute later, an air force ground controller got him the message that he was targeting the wrong airplane.

By this time, the suspect airplane was landing on a grass runway in the jungles of Colombia. We radioed in the coordinates and departed the area. There was nothing more we could do, and I wasn't going to give this knucklehead fighter pilot another chance at me.

I have often been asked how these kinds of situations affected me. Did I have a death wish? How did I cope continually working in such dangerous environments?

This might be a good time to tell you my thoughts on these matters. First of all, I don't have a death wish. I want to live as long as anyone else does. It's just that, as a Christian, I know where I'm going after I die, so death doesn't worry me. I've heard the saying, "everybody wants to go to heaven but nobody wants to die." Well I don't worry about the dying part either. I believe that everyone has a certain amount of time to live, and it doesn't matter if you are at home in a recliner watching television or flying jets over Colombian jungles with people shooting at you. When it's your time, it's your time.

I have seen too many friends die who did everything right. They lived normal, peaceful lives. They ate well and exercised regularly and then they suddenly died. I've seen other friends who did wild and crazy things that should have killed them a hundred times. They drank too much and ate all the wrong foods. They wouldn't even know how to spell exercise. Yet these people are still kicking. I can explain this no other way than to say that our days are numbered when we are born.

When you run out of days, then time's up, you're dead. It doesn't matter what you're doing.

When I'm faced with a life or death situation, I get a little excited. I'm thinking, "In the next minute I'm going to see a miracle. I'm either going to be standing in front of God, or he is going to perform a miracle to get me out of this situation. Either way, I'm going to see a miracle."

Of course, I don't always take surviving for granted. It just might be my time to die. I remember a story about a man who was on a boat that sank in the middle of the ocean. He found himself treading water, along with several other people who had been on the boat. He prayed for God to save him. A short time later, a rescue boat appeared beside him and someone yelled for him to get aboard, there was only room for one more.

He looked around him and saw others who were struggling to stay afloat more than he was. He yelled to the rescue boat, "No, I can swim a little longer. Save that person over there instead." The rescue boat went over and picked up the other person. Soon a helicopter arrived and threw him a line. He looked over and noticed a lady next to him who was just about to drown. He handed her the line. The helicopter could hold no more people and it departed.

After a while, the man drowned. When he got to heaven, he was met by God. God shook his hand and welcomed him to heaven. God asked, "Before I show you around, do you have any questions?" The man said, "Just one. Why didn't you save me after I prayed to you?" God looked at him with a puzzled face and said, "What do you mean? I sent you a boat and a helicopter!"

After my stint in Colombia, it was time to go to Peru. I was actually on the very first Citation crew deployed to Peru, so I didn't know what to expect. I knew one thing: it was a long way down there. I departed Howard AFB, flew over Bogotá, Colombia, crossed over the equator, and, a thousand miles later, landed in Iquitos, Peru.

Iquitos was like an island surrounded by land. It was a city of four hundred thousand people carved out of triple-canopy jungle on the bank of the Amazon River. There were only two ways into that place, by air or by boat. It was so far in the jungle that no roadways led in or out. The nearest town was over a hundred miles away.

Most of the local people were half a generation away from living in grass huts in the jungle. In fact, I met a lot of them who used to live that way. Twenty miles to the south, there were still natives who looked just like photos you've seen in *National Geographic* magazines. I know because I've visited a village and seen the bare-breasted women wearing skirts made of tree bark and all. Only twenty years before, an explorer was eaten by cannibals in this area. One of the pilots told me he was convinced that dinosaurs still lived in these jungles.

To visit the native village required a trip down the Amazon River in a small boat. The guide my crew and I had hired stopped along the bank and cut some limbs off of a tree. We used them as fishing poles. I wanted to catch a piranha. The river was full of them, and I wanted to say that I had caught one.

It was a lot easier said than done. The piranhas kept eating the bait off the hooks but wouldn't bite the hook. It was hot, so for some reason I decided to jump in the Amazon River. If I couldn't say I had caught a piranha, I could at least say I had swum with them. I jumped in and went under until I touched the bottom. It was a gooey mud that gave me the creeps. I swam back and got into the boat. On the way back to Iquitos, the boat driver told me that a young native child had been eaten by piranhas a few months earlier.

The airport at Iquitos only had a single runway that had grass growing out of the countless cracks. The first time I landed there, I almost hit some kids who lived only about a hundred feet away. They played ball on the runway when planes weren't landing.

The hotel we stayed in on the first few trips was called the El Dorado, named after the fictional lost city of gold. Or was it fiction? I would have to research this more. There were few cars in the city. Everyone had these three-wheel motorcycle looking things. I don't think there were any traffic laws, and a person crossing the street only had a fifty-fifty shot at surviving.

Finding a place to eat was always a challenge. I came close to starving there. I've never been in a place with such awful food. One pilot opened a can and filled it half-full of sand. Then he drained some jet fuel into it and mixed it up. It was a jerry-rigged steno can. When he lit it, it produced a small flame that he used to cook Spam. The only problem was, it smoked a lot and left black soot over everything. I know this because he tried it in his hotel room and his walls and ceiling were covered in black soot.

We did find a restaurant down on the bank of the Amazon that had edible food. It also had an amazing view overlooking the world's largest river. Being from New Orleans, I was a little skeptical when I was first seated at this restaurant in an outside area that only had a thatched roof and was built right over the edge of the Amazon. I mean, the view was great, but on the Mississippi River in New Orleans, if you sit out like that mosquitoes will eat you up. I had already been warned that the mosquitoes there carried all kind of diseases. But I had taken a dozen different shots before I left home, and I was taking malaria pills. I couldn't imagine any disease I wasn't vaccinated against, so I sat down.

I noticed clear plastic baggies filled with water hanging from the ceiling throughout the room. I found out that this was a jungle-style mosquito repellent. Sunlight hitting the water in the bags created a reflection that scared away the mosquitoes. It actually worked. I never saw a mosquito in there. I didn't go at night.

Flying patrols over the Amazon jungle was different, but I like different. The land around Iquitos was flat. Flying over this flat, triple-canopy jungle from the perspective of the airplane looked just like flying over the ocean, except it was green instead of blue. For hundreds of square miles, there was nothing but a flat layer of green. The only thing breaking up the constant green was the Amazon River as it wound through the jungle. While patrolling at night, I could see no lights from the cities below, only occasional campfires along the river. Maybe my friend was right, maybe dinosaurs did still live here.

We were here because of what we called the Peruvian-Colombian corridor. Most of the coca plants were grown in Peru and then flown into Colombia to be processed into cocaine. We figured that if we could stop planes from delivering the coca plants to the coke labs, we could drastically cut down on cocaine production.

Since there were few roads in northern Peru, the roads could easily be controlled. So there was no way for the smugglers to drive to Colombia. They also couldn't get to Colombia by water, at least not efficiently. So, shutting down the air corridor was a high priority for both the Peruvian and United States governments.

Just like the Colombians, the Peruvians were using their air force to shoot down smugglers' airplanes. Once again, foreign fighter jets were flying off our wing, and we were guiding them to the targets. They, too, lacked radar and night vision capabilities. There was one big difference between them and the Colombians—they couldn't speak *any* English! Of course, my Spanish language skills were horrible. I must have spent at least two years in Spanish speaking countries and never learned more than five words. I knew I would never learn Spanish, so I would just have to stick with the two languages I knew, English and Southern. Truthfully, my English wasn't all that good either.

My first time working with a Peruvian fighter almost got me killed, which is probably not unexpected. We were doing a practice intercept flight. I just wanted the fighter to intercept us in the Citation and join us in formation. Then we would do a few turns and altitude changes, simulating chasing a smuggler. Very simple stuff, and since it was the first time flying together, we did it in broad daylight.

I could see in my FLIR screen the A-37 approaching at my six o'clock. He was coming fast, too fast. He was supposed to join me and fly about fifty feet off my right wingtip. He kept getting closer and closer at a high rate of speed and at the same altitude. Now, he should have been about five hundred feet below me until he was stabilized in position. Then he could move up and join me in formation. But no! He kept coming, but he descended at the last moment and flew directly under me. He was flying at least a hundred knots faster than I was flying. He zoomed past the Citation, missing us by mere feet. He had totally screwed up the intercept and almost crashed into me.

After a few tries he finally managed to get into formation, but he stayed at least five hundred feet away. That was okay with me. If all the Peruvian pilots flew like this, I was a little worried about them intercepting me at night. Luckily, I never had to guide them in to shoot down an airplane. Another New Orleans crew did. The pilot told me the story and it was screwed up, just as I imagined it would be.

They had picked up a target at night. It was illegal to fly at night in Peru, so there was no doubt this plane was a smuggler. It was well advertised that planes flying at night were subject to being shot down. In addition, this plane was flying with its lights out. That's another big no-no.

The New Orleans Citation intercepted the target and called in the fighter. Now, there were rules of engagement that everyone was to follow. The rules were that we were to try to communicate with the suspect airplane. If we could get it to land, that was a lot better than shooting it down. Since we did not know Spanish, it was up to the fighter pilot to do the communicating.

If that didn't work, the fighter would shoot some tracer rounds in front of the airplane to warn the pilot to land or be shot down. Tracers are bullets that glow and leave a trail behind them so they are very visible at night. Shooting down an airplane was always the last resort.

The Citation directed in the fighter, expecting it to follow the rules of engagement and try to communicate. As soon as the fighter got sight of the airplane, it opened fire directly into the airplane. The suspect plane burst into flames, spun down, and crashed. The whole thing took less than a minute. No attempt at communicating, no warning shots, just bang-bang you're dead.

When that plane crashed, it created a huge fireball. The Citation marked the spot. To give you an idea just how thick the jungle was, the next day, the Peruvians sent out a helicopter to check the wreckage. Even with the exact latitude and longitude, it took two days for the helicopter to find it. The triple-canopy jungle just swallowed it up.

After that event, customs pilots told the US policy makers that it was just a matter of time before an innocent airplane was accidently shot down. Of course, no one listened until it was too late. Less than a year after the shoot-down policy was enacted, our worst-case scenario happened. I'm glad I wasn't there at the time. In fact, there was not even a customs airplane involved. There was another US agency in Peru doing the same mission we were doing, but they didn't have the experience that we had.

Their plane picked up a target just after dark and did the normal intercept procedures. A Peruvian fighter was vectored into the trail of the suspect. This time, the plane seemed to be heading for Iquitos, and the agency pilots told the fighter not to shoot until they could positively identify the suspect airplane.

Unknown to the agency or fighter pilots, while this intercept was going on, the pilot of the suspect airplane was talking to air traffic controllers in Iquitos. He was planning to land there. For some reason, the fighter pilot was not calling on the proper frequency. Since the plane was heading directly for Iquitos, the fighter should have at least have called them to see if they were in contract with the plane.

Despite the agency crew telling it not to shoot, the fighter opened fire. I guess it's possible, with the language communications problem they were having, that the fighter pilot didn't understand what they were saying. But for whatever reason, he shot the plane down. It turned out to be some missionaries.

This made headlines around the world and started an international investigation into the whole shoot-down policy. Until then, it had been a secret, classified project. Of course, there was little defense, and soon the shoot-down policy was ended, both in Peru and Colombia. With no end game, it wasn't long before customs pulled out of both countries.

CHAPTER FIFTEEN

The next country I visited was Honduras. It was about a three-hour Citation flight north of Howard Air Force Base in Panama. We would depart Howard and fly over the Pacific Ocean until we reached Honduras. If the skies were clear, we always used a large volcano as a landmark to show us where to turn east into Honduras. It was a perfect example of what you would think a volcano should look like.

It rose up five thousand feet from the Pacific coastline in a perfectly formed mountain. It had a round crater in the middle of its sunken top that was filled with clear blue water. A magnificent sight that could only be fully appreciated from the air.

Honduras was a poor but beautiful country. I visited a lake there that was surrounded by hills and looked very much like a lake I used to fish on in Tennessee. There were also two huge waterfalls on a river running through the mountains that I explored. Having never been up close to a big waterfall, I had not realized how much noise they made.

Driving through the countryside was depressing. For miles and miles, the houses along the road had no electricity or running water. A lot of the houses had thatched roofs. I passed over a bridge on a small river and saw dozens of people washing their clothes in the muddy water.

It reminded me of a sight I saw daily in Iquitos. On the drive to the airport, we passed a large garbage dump. At this dump, we saw people, including children, fighting the birds for food scraps. Unless you've traveled out of the country, you cannot realize how blessed we are to live in America.

Our living quarters on the Soto Canto Air Base was a double-wide mobile home that customs had brought in just for us. It had the only bathtub on the base, and the female soldiers were jealous. The only bad part about the trailer was that it was placed too close to the base's perimeter fence. There were some anti-government factions in Honduras who were in the habit of throwing grenades over the fence of the base.

I don't think I ever launched on a real target while in Honduras. In theory, it was a good location to intercept northbound targets, but it just never developed into a productive location.

The United States, being the kind-hearted and caring nation we are, decided to turn over control of the Panama Canal to the Panamanian government. This turnover included giving them Howard Air Force Base. I was still flying in and out of Howard during this sad time. The air force had spent a fortune fixing up the base—just to hand it over to Panama. No wonder our country is broke.

After control of the Canal was in the hands of the Panamanians, there were hundreds of ships backed up on both sides trying to get through the canal. I guess running the canal effectively was not as easy as they had anticipated. It was totally screwed up for over a year. But the world was still happy, because big, bad America was no longer in charge. Give me a break!

Before I stop talking about Panama, I've got to tell you one more quick story. Believe it or not, I'm fully capable of making an occasional stupid decision. After spending thirty days working out of Central and South America, I was always ready to go home. After one particularly difficult thirty-day rotation, I was going home, no matter what the weather. Never mind if there was a hurricane between Panama and New Orleans!

I checked the weather carefully and found it was only a Category 1 hurricane, with cloud tops only thirty-five thousand feet or less. The Citation can fly at over forty thousand feet, so I didn't see a problem flying over this minor little hurricane. It wasn't but a couple of hundred miles across, anyway. I discussed it with my crew, and everyone agreed. We all wanted to go home. If we waited, the hurricane could turn into the Gulf of Mexico and head for Louisiana. If that happened, we could be stranded in Panama for another week.

We took off and headed home. The weather turned out to be just as I had hoped. We never flew into a single cloud and never experienced any turbulence whatsoever. Flying over the top, I enjoyed the view of a hurricane from this perspective. I was thinking to myself what a good decision I had made to fly home. Then, suddenly it dawned on me. What if we had to make an emergency landing, or lost pressurization, or had to ditch? There would be no one able to come and rescue us. We would be on our own for countless hours in the middle of a hurricane.

Flying over that hurricane had been a really dumb decision. But now that I think about it, maybe the co-pilot had talked me into it. I never wanted to do it in the first place. You believe me don't you?

The smugglers were beginning to airdrop their drugs into Haiti and the Dominican Republic. Venezuela was beginning to replace Colombia as the country where the smugglers' airplanes originated. To counter this new threat US Customs made one of the best decisions they have ever made: they started deploying Citation crews to Aruba. I say this with a smile on my face, of course. Aruba is one of the most beautiful and fun places that I have ever been assigned to.

Aruba was a Dutch-owned jewel of an island located in the Caribbean, about forty miles north of Venezuela. They put us humble pilots in a great hotel on a gorgeous beach. Since the Europeans are a little more opened-minded than most of the world, in Aruba, women sunbathers could go topless. It was just one of those unpleasant difficulties I would have to endure for my country. The hotel had a casino and, thank goodness, a restaurant with great food.

Aruba had a climate that I had never experienced before. It was called a tropical desert. There is actually a desert on an island in the Caribbean Sea. Go figure. I found a cave while exploring the island that had hundreds of people's names carved into the rock walls. Some dated back to the 1700s. I guess there were a lot of other people who liked to explore the island too. I found out later that the cave had poisonous centipedes in it. What the heck? Might as well add that to my list.

It was a beautiful area to fly our patrols. I got to see all the islands in the south part of the Caribbean that I had missed while flying out of Puerto Rico. The only thing we had to watch out for was flying too close to Venezuela. They were threatening to shoot us down if we flew into their airspace.

The usual route the smugglers would take was to depart Venezuela and fly up to the Dominican Republic to airdrop their drugs. Then they would fly back into Venezuela and land. We chased them all day long, but without the political will to shoot them down, there was nothing we could do.

There were times when we would chase them north as they came out of Venezuela until our fuel was low. Then a navy plane or customs plane based in Puerto Rico would take the handoff from us. They would follow the smugglers to Haiti or the Dominican Republic and watch them airdrop to a boat or inside one of these countries and then fly back south. We would refuel and pick the target up again and follow it back to Venezuela. Venezuela would not let us fly into their airspace and would not allow their law enforcement to respond, so this million dollars spent chasing the smuggler was for nothing.

The law enforcement authorities in Haiti or the Dominican Republic usually did not attempt to make any arrests or seize the dope. It all depended on who had paid off the right people. But I didn't let this ridiculous waste of time and money bother me. I was getting used to it by now. Besides, I was living on the beach of Aruba!

The smugglers were also using fast boats to smuggle their drugs. They were specially modified long and narrow boats that sat very low in the water. It was almost impossible to pick them up on radar. On our patrols, we would look for the wake of these boats as they streaked northward at sixty miles per hour. We couldn't see the boats but we could sure see their wake. That is, if the seas were calm.

I was on a patrol one night when a navy ship called me about a boat target that they had been watching. It had dropped its load and was heading back to Colombia. Unlike Venezuela, if we could determine what port in Colombia the boat was going to, there was a slight chance that the officials would actually do something about it.

I picked up the wake of the boat and began following it into Colombia. Soon it was evident that I was either going to have to return to Aruba for fuel and forget about the boat or continue chasing the boat and refuel in Colombia. Refueling in Colombia was always a hit-or-miss kind of thing. Between the drug cartels and the civil war going on, we never knew what airport was safe to land at. Our command center had to contact the American Embassy in Colombia and ask them to make some calls to get approval for me to refuel. All this took time, of course, especially in the middle of the night.

Meanwhile, I was getting to the point of breaking off the target and returning to Aruba. In the end, the pilot-in-command of the airplane had the final word as to the safety of the airplane. The bureaucrats could take all the time they wanted, but I wasn't going to run out of fuel waiting.

Finally, the approval came for me to refuel in Colombia. This allowed me to stay with the boat until it pulled into port. I radioed all the information to the appropriate people. I would never know if the Colombians responded to the boat. We almost never knew.

I landed at an Colombian airport in Barranquilla. I was directed to taxi to a certain spot, and, as I was shutting down the airplane's engines, a military truck approached and parked in front of me. About ten soldiers jumped out of the back with rifles and surrounded the Citation. It was like déjà vu all over again.

I was wondering if I was at the right airport, or whether maybe the Embassy had somehow screwed up. Before we could get out of the airplane, a fuel truck pulled up and began pumping fuel in the plane. After we got out and started talking to the officer in charge, he told us that the soldiers were for our protection. That it wasn't safe around here. No kidding! We fueled up and got out of there as soon as we could.

I think I went to Aruba five or six times before customs decided to move operations to some other place. After all, Aruba was way too nice a location for customs pilots to be hanging around.

I was back in the United States and back in the Gulf of Mexico doing a radar patrol, watching the screen on my air-to-air radar. It was giving some indications that I had never seen before. It is a very complex piece of equipment, so I thought that maybe it was just some electrons running amok.

It was locking up a target that was traveling over fifteen hundred miles per hour. What was interesting was that I had just recently watched a show on television about an F-16 fighter jet in Germany whose radar had picked up the same type of target. The TV show even showed a recording of the radar screen and it looked exactly like the indications I was seeing on mine. It only lasted a short time, then it was gone.

On the TV show they had speculated that the target was a UFO. In all my flying I've never seen a UFO, but I did believe there was something out there that was flying at an incredible rate of speed. A few days later, I may have discovered the answer to this phenomenon.

I was in my office at the Belle Chase Navy Base when someone came in and said that a SR-71 airplane had just landed. I jumped up from my desk and ran outside with all the other pilots. The SR-71 was a secret spy plane that could fly at incredible altitudes and airspeeds. We had all read about them and seen pictures of them but none of us had ever seen one up close.

The SR-71 taxied to a hangar only about two hundred yards from the customs ramp and was quickly surrounded by air force security guards. It was towed inside the hangar and the hangar door was shut. It turns out that the plane had had an engine failure over the Gulf of Mexico, and this was the closest airport in which to land. If this airplane had been flying over the Gulf a few days earlier, then I had my explanation of the strange radar indications. The SR-71 was fully capable of flying over fifteen hundred miles per hour.

One of the customs pilots was in the navy reserves and knew the people who worked in this hangar. The next day, he walked over and talked to one of the mechanics who was working on replacing the engine. He was told by the mechanic that he had never seen an engine like this before. The turbine blades inside the engine would feather at a certain airspeed and altitude, and the engine would turn from a turbine engine into a ram jet engine.

This airplane had an interesting history. It was actually built back in the late fifties and early sixties, yet could still out-fly any aircraft in the sky. They only made a limited number of them and then supposedly destroyed the blueprints so they could never be built again. I always felt that was kind of strange, but another customs pilot told me a story that was even stranger.

He was an ex-air force pilot who was once stationed at Wright-Patterson Air Force Base. He had a friend who worked there as a military policeman. His friend was frequently assigned to guard a hangar that was always locked. Whatever was in the hangar was considered top secret. His friend had gotten to know one of the people who worked inside the hangar and was told by that person that inside was the spacecraft that had crashed in Roswell, Arizona.

I am sure you all know the story about the UFO that supposedly crashed in Roswell, Arizona in the 1950s. There have been countless television shows about this crash. I have seen several of them, and they all said that the evidence suggested the spacecraft had been moved to the Wright-Patterson Air Force Base. Could this customs pilot's story have some truth to it? The customs pilot told me that he had heard that advanced technology had been used from the UFO to build the SR-71. I don't know if I believed this story. I do know that the building of the SR-71 used incredibly advanced technology that was way beyond what was generally available at the time. In fact, fifty years later, we still cannot build an aircraft like the SR-71.

I was lucky enough to be in the office a few days later when they pulled the SR-71 out of the hangar and performed a maintenance test flight. I watched it take off and make several trips around the airport, testing the new engine. From a distance, the profile of the airplane looked just like an UFO. I can see now why some people may have thought this was a flying saucer.

On the last pass around the airport, the SR-71 turned its nose straight up, lit its afterburners, and disappeared within seconds, straight up into the clear blue sky. It was an incredible sight. Most of these aircraft are now retired, and you can see them at museums around the country. But they were still very secret and mysterious the week that I had my close encounter.

When we chased suspects in the Citation, we would often have to fly just above stall speed. This was especially dangerous in a jet because it took more time to recover the airplane if you did accidently stall. To teach us to better handle these unusual attitude situations, customs decided to send some of us instructors to an aerobatic training course they called "upset training."

The training was held in central Florida and was given by one of the world's top aerobatic pilots. It was great training, with the goal of teaching us how to survive the low-level, unusual attitudes we could possibly encounter on low-speed Citation chases.

The airplane we used was called an Extra 300, one of the best aerobatic airplanes available. It was capable of doing a lot more high G maneuvers than my body was. We did all kinds of aerobatic stunts that I had seen at countless air shows. On the last day we did a "Lomcevak," a very complex maneuver that has the airplane flipping end over end at all kinds of weird angles. That was the big attraction at all the air shows, but only a few pilots in the world could perform it.

The aerobatic pilot giving me this instruction died a few months later while performing at an air show in Miami. He was attempting to set a world record on the number of spins by an airplane.

About this same time, a New Orleans customs pilot was promoted to commanding officer of a Louisiana Air National Guard Unit, based a mile down the road from my office. This unit flew F-15 fighter jets. I had watched them taking off in awe ever since I had arrived at the navy base. I never dreamed I would get to fly one, but after ten years of begging, suddenly things came together just right, and I was scheduled for a flight.

Not just anyone can get a flight in one of the world's top fighter jets. There has to be a good reason for the air force to allow a civilian to fly it. It took me and the CO of the unit ten years to come up with a good enough reason to make it happen. And that reason was pretty funny.

I had recently written a fiction book called *Sky Warrior* about the war on drugs. It was about a rogue customs pilot going up against a Colombian drug cartel. In the book, I had discussed using military aircraft to assist customs in winning the drug war. My friend, who is now a full-time general for the Guard, took this book with him on a trip to the Pentagon. Somehow he convinced them that they should fly me in the status of a reporter/writer who would tell America about the role the air force plays in the war on drugs. Brains like that are why he made general.

I had to train for hours before the flight. The main thing was learning to operate the ejection seat. Finally, the day arrived for me to fly, and it should have been a warning to me when I was told to eat six Tums antacids before the flight and not to eat breakfast.

We started our takeoff roll on full afterburners and were airborne by halfway down the runway. But instead of a normal climb, the pilot leveled the jet about ten feet off the ground. We accelerated in ground effect and reached over three hundred fifty miles per hour by the end of the runway. He then pulled up the nose of the F-15 and we shot straight up like a rocket to over ten thousand feet. When I say like a rocket, I mean it. The F-15 had set the world climb record to fifty thousand feet. It can reach that altitude faster than a Saturn Five rocket.

When we had reached about twelve thousand feet, he rolled the airplane upside down and I looked straight down at the airport where we had been five seconds ago. We headed the fighter to a military practice area out in the Gulf of Mexico. About one minute into the flight, he gave me the controls and about thirty seconds later I was doing rolls.

I have flown more than thirty different types of airplanes and helicopters and I found the F-15 to be a very stable and easy airplane to fly. Of course, that was straight and level flying without using all the sophisticated radar and weapons systems on the plane. To fly the plane in a dogfight, shooting missiles and guns, requires a great deal of skill and training. We flew out into the practice area and did all kinds of maneuvers such as flying straight up, straight down, simulating bombing runs, and high G turns.

I soon discovered why they had asked me to eat so many Tums. I was quickly getting airsick as we performed the high G maneuvers. I didn't throw up, but I sure came close. A "G" is the equivalent of the weight of gravity. If you weighed two hundred pounds, at one G you still weighed two hundred pounds. But at five Gs you felt like you weighed a thousand pounds. We pulled 6.7 Gs that day. Flying fighters is definitely a young man's game.

Then we did what I had always dreamed of doing, flying faster than the speed of sound. It was a little underwhelming. My expectation had been a little more. I'm not sure what I was expecting but if I hadn't been looking at the airspeed indicator I would never have known we were flying above Mach 1. I guess technology has come a long way since the Chuck Yeager days, when breaking the sound barrier caused the airplane to do all sorts of crazy things.

Up high in the air it is hard to get a true reference of how fast you're really traveling. I wanted to get a sensation of just how fast this bird really was, so we dropped down to about five hundred feet off the ground. Flying over the swamps of Louisiana, we kicked it up to just below the speed of sound. We couldn't legally fly above Mach 1 over land. If we had, the sonic boom would have broken windows in every building for miles around.

Now, I had the need for speed. With the glass canopy on the F-15, the pilots get the feeling of riding on the top of a rocket. This thing made the Citation feel like riding a tricycle. I was going to have to buy me one of these. If only I had about thirty million dollars.

The flight was by far the best flight I have ever taken. And to make it even more special I crossed over my ten-thousandth flight hour while flying faster than the speed of sound. Very cool! I had purposely timed this flight to coincide with my ten-thousandth hour. A few years later, I would cross over my eleven-thousandth flight hour while flying over Baghdad in a US Army spy plane.

Since I was doing all this extreme flying, I decided I wanted to make a parachute jump. Despite all the flying I had done, I had never parachuted. I was visiting family in Florida, who just happened to be close to one of the country's largest jump schools. I went over one day and signed up. Before they would let me jump alone, I had to do what they called a tandem jump, which meant I had to jump attached to a jump instructor first.

After a few minutes of training, I was ready to go. We got on the airplane and climbed up to twelve thousand feet. We would free fall (without opening the chute) until five thousand feet, then open the chute and glide back to the place we had taken off from. Safe enough, right? My instructor had done it seventeen hundred times without a single problem. But he had never jumped with me!

The airplane was a fairly large plane, with a large door that opened in the back, sort of like a garage door. It was open, and we walked over to the edge. I was one step away from a two-mile drop. I thought I might be a little nervous, but I guess I was too accustomed to flying. I was ready to go without a second's hesitation.

We jumped from the plane and it was just as much fun as I thought it would be. We fell from the sky at over a hundred and twenty miles an hour. At five thousand feet, the jump instructor pulled the cord to open the parachute. It didn't open! At least it didn't open properly. It was what parachutist called a streamer. The chute came out of the pack but did not inflate like it was suppose to. Looking up at it, it was just a ball of fabric and tangled cords. It wasn't slowing us down at all and the ground was coming fast. We had waited to the last minute to deploy the chute.

The instructor knew just what to do and jettisoned the malfunctioning parachute. Now we were free falling again, and I didn't want to even guess at how close to the ground we were. He pulled the cord of the reserve chute, and luckily it opened perfectly. It was a good thing. You almost didn't have this book to read.

After a quick break back on the ground I was getting set to make my solo jump. If the instructor had made seventeen hundred jumps with only this one problem, I figured the odds were pretty good the next jump would go well. Am I right or am I being a little overly optimistic?

This time, there were six other jumpers in the plane with us. We would all jump together. The instructor would stay beside me during the free fall in case I screwed something up. Then we would separate, and I would pull my ripcord and float gently down from the sky. You probably know by now that wasn't going to happen.

We jumped from the plane and everything seemed perfect to me. But instead of me opening my chute at 5,000 feet as we planned, the instructor gave me a hand signal to open it at 6,000 feet. With no time to reason why, my only choice was to do or die. I pulled the chute and it opened as advertized. See, I told you. But we did have a problem. The winds had shifted and the airplane had dropped us in the wrong location to make it back to the airport.

That was unless you had a lot of helicopter flight time and you had a steerable parachute. I adjusted the chute and set up a glide angle, just as if I was landing a helicopter, and I glided right down to spot we had planned. The instructor followed beside me, so he made it back too. All of the other parachutist landed in fields more than a mile away. It had been a fun day, and I could finally say that I had jumped out of a perfectly good airplane. But it would be more than ten years later before I tried it again.

CHAPTER SIXTEEN

Once again, the smugglers changed their tactics. We had been so successful in stopping them from entering the United States by airplane that they began flying their dope into Mexico. Then they would smuggle it across the US/Mexican border by vehicle or in the backpack of a person walking across.

US Customs started deploying aircraft and crews to Mexico. On each of our flights in the beginning, we put a "host nation rider," which was a pilot who was in the PGR, in the cockpit. The PGR was the Mexican version of our FBI. The rationale behind this was to help train the Mexican pilots so that, eventually, they could fly their own airplanes on intercept missions.

It also helped to have a Spanish speaker aboard and someone with the authority to call for assistance with any local law enforcement officers or with the military. But the real reason was political. It gave the Mexican government a little control over what we were doing. It was the whole sovereign nation thing. We wouldn't want Mexican law enforcement officers flying over the United States unless we were keeping a close eye on them, after all.

The biggest problem I had, and all the other customs pilots felt the same way, was that they couldn't fly! They had never flown an airplane as complex as the Citation. On my first flight with a PGR pilot, I let him do the flying. I was a Citation instructor, so I felt comfortable letting him handle the controls, and I wanted to know just how good of a pilot he was.

On the first landing, he came in very high and over a hundred miles an hour too fast. I tried to tell him to adjust, but he continued toward the runway. We had that language barrier problem again. We had been assured that all the PGR pilots were fluent in English. Eventually, I had to take the controls to keep from crashing. At the recommendations of several of us customs pilots, they made it a policy that the PGR pilots could only fly as co-pilots.

The smugglers would often fly from Colombia, up the western coastline of Central America, and Mexico, and get as close to the American border as they thought was safe. Then they would land at a dirt airstrip to offload their dope. A good location to base the Citation, in order to intercept these planes, turned out to be Puerto Vallarta.

Puerto Vallarta is a beautiful resort city on the Pacific Ocean. Customs was getting better at picking our living quarters. We stayed there in a four-star hotel suite right on the beach. Every day, if I wasn't flying, I would go out to the pool and watch the sun set into the Pacific Ocean.

A few miles from the hotel, there was a bullfighting stadium, and once I went to watch the bullfight. It was a lot bloodier and crueler to the bulls than I had anticipated. I still enjoyed it, but it is one of those things you only like to do once.

About ten miles outside the city, there was this very cool little restaurant up in the mountains that we all enjoyed. It was where Arnold Schwarzenegger had filmed a scene from the movie *Predator*. Another cool thing I did while I was there was to rent a boat and go whale watching.

Puerto Vallarta was definitely a cool place to stay, and we even got into some good airplane chases. I got a call once that radar had been tracking a suspect airplane flying up from the south Pacific, and the controllers requested that we intercept. I got airborne in the Citation and pointed it in the right direction. By that time, a PGR King Air was also launching to join the chase. We intercepted the target just as it passed Puerto Vallarta.

It was dark, but we could see with the infrared that it was a large airplane. The smugglers had been using much larger planes lately to transport their loads from Colombia to Mexico. I guess they figured it was safe for them to do so. Of course, they didn't know that I was in the country. Ha! Just joking. They didn't know that customs had put airplanes in Mexico to assist the PGR. At least, we didn't think they knew. Well, tonight they would get a rude awakening.

There was no need to get close enough to get the registration number off the tail of the airplane. There was no doubt it was a smuggler. It had departed Colombia, was on no flight plan, and was not talking to any air traffic controllers. So it didn't matter about the tail number, we were going to land behind it and check it out anyway. Actually, let me be perfectly correct with that statement. The PGR and the Mexican military were going to land behind it and check it out. We had no authority to arrest anyone in Mexico. Customs was there to assist and advise only.

The plane I was chasing was a Gulfstream 1. It was a large turbo-prop twin engine airplane that had been used as a commuter airliner twenty years earlier. It could seat forty people, and, with the seats removed, it could transport tons of illegal narcotics. Customs had never caught a big load of drugs like that before in an airplane, and I was hoping to be the first to do it.

We had been following this plane for hours, and we began to worry about fuel. Our tanks were getting low, but we didn't want to break off the target and possibly lose it. Since we were in a part of Mexico that I'd never been to before, I was busy flying. I asked the PGR pilot, who was now flying as co-pilot, to locate an airport where we could refuel. I knew there were few places where we could get jet fuel in the middle of the night, and the last thing I needed was to get stranded for the night on some remote Mexican airport in Indian territory.

He knew his country better than I did, and since he sure wasn't helping fly the plane, at least he could find a place to refuel. But that seemed to be too much to expect. After about the tenth time that I asked him where we could land, I placed my hand on his shoulder and told him to look me in the eyes.

I told him that I was going to break off the chase if he didn't tell me where to get fuel. I had to know so that I could determine how much longer we could stay in the chase. He finally got the message and showed me on the map, or as aviators say "aeronautical chart," where we could land. I calculated that we could remain in the chase a while longer.

It wasn't a language problem that was keeping him from answering me. He was busy on the radio talking with the PGR King Air that was also in the chase. The Mexicans seemed unfamiliar with radio discipline. Whenever they were on the radio, they engaged in a nonstop tirade of excited yelling that gave me a headache. I couldn't understand a single word, but I could not image what in the world they had to talk about. It didn't help that in Spanish you have to say three words for every one in English to get the same point across.

The PGR King Air did not have night vision capabilities, so it was supposed to be in trail behind me. I had all the lights off on the Citation except one tiny light on the tail. That light had been especially designed so aircraft could use it to follow behind. I was a mile behind the G-1 and it was dark, so the only way I could see it was with the infrared camera.

Suddenly, an airplane flew right in front of the Citation, between me and the G-1. It was a near miss, or what it should be called a near hit. I never saw it out the window, just on the infrared screen. It turned out to be the Mexican King Air. For some reason, which I'll never know until the day I learn Spanish, the King Air pilot wanted to take a closer look at the G-1. Maybe he didn't like me being in the lead. Anyway, he nearly killed us all.

Looking back on those days, it's a wonder that more customs pilots didn't get killed, myself included. A couple of years later, after we thought we had trained their pilots, the US government gave the Mexicans a Citation. Within six months, they had crashed it.

Just after the near miss, the G-1 started to descend. I think it had seen the King Air, but for whatever reason, it was preparing to land. We checked the map and there were no airports anywhere close, so maybe it was landing on a dirt airstrip the smugglers had made. But when it got down low to the ground, it didn't land—it started evasive maneuvers designed to shake anyone following it. Now I knew the smugglers had seen the King Air!

Trying to chase the G-1 through the mountains at night could have been very dangerous, except for one thing: With the air-to-air radar and FLIR we had, we didn't need to fly low. We could stay at a safe altitude and still keep track of it. Isn't modern technology great?

Soon the plane started circling as if it was looking for a place to land. By this time, we also had three Mexican Army helicopters in the chase. If this mission went well, it might restore my faith in the Mexican government. At least it seemed that they were putting in a valiant effort.

The G-1 was on a final decent to what looked like a farmer's field. We could see nowhere for it to land on the infrared camera. I was circling overhead and watching it on the FLIR screen as it touched down. It veered to the right and one of the main landing gear wheels broke off the airplane. It then suddenly turned ninety degrees and disappeared into a cloud of smoke. No wait a second, it was a cloud of dust. Looks the same in infrared.

A minute later we saw the door open. Five people ran out of the airplane. Maybe they were afraid it was about to burst onto flames. The helicopters were still about ten minutes out. We had been flying too fast for them to stay in formation. While we were waiting, we watched five smugglers run into a ditch.

Once they were in the ditch, they kept running up the ditch at breakneck speed. It was funny to watch. The ditch was covered with heavy trees and I'm sure they thought they could escape. But of course they didn't know that customs was overhead with a new infrared toy. Hey smugglers, you can run but you can't hide!

When the army helicopters arrived, we guided them to the runners. Not only did we see them capture the five smugglers, we also recorded the incident on video tape as the smugglers were loaded into the helicopters. I promise you it's true. The reason I'm making such a fuss is because the next day the Mexicans claimed they had only found one person!

The G-1 was loaded with over eighteen thousand pounds of cocaine. Who knows for sure how much was really on it. I somehow didn't believe the official Mexican report. That was like $100 million in street value. There is another significant thing about this load was: It was the largest airplane drug seizure in customs history. I had done it! I had made history! But it didn't count. I couldn't claim it because we were in Mexico, remember.

On another day, I was asked to check on a suspicious boat that had been spotted by a navy vessel. Since we were putting a lot of pressure on the smugglers, they were trying a new route. Instead of following the shoreline, this boat was two hundred miles offshore. I'm not sure if the person in our control center who requested the launch realized how far the target was from Puerto Vallarta.

When I checked it out, it was over nine hundred miles away. A little more planning helped me to determine that if I refueled in Acapulco, the trip was doable. I had always wanted to see Acapulco, since I had only seen it in the movies, when Elvis had dived off the cliffs there. So who was I to tell anyone how far away this target was? I was just following orders. It was a very long day. The boat turned out to be legal, but I got to see Acapulco. I even flew over the famous cliffs, so I guess the trip was worth it.

After things quieted down along the Pacific coast we started deploying to Monterrey, Mexico. This was in the northeast part of the country. The smugglers were landing up close to the border and driving the dope across.

Customs put us in an old but nice hotel in the downtown area. The hotel had been remodeled, but it was almost a hundred years old. It had a colorful history. Poncho Villa, the famous Mexican revolutionary hero, had once stayed there. In fact, he had ridden his horse up the large spiral stairway in the lobby and put it in the room next to his.

They told us it was safe there, but they assigned us an armored, bulletproof vehicle to drive. This thing was brand new and even had its own air supply. In case of a chemical attack, we could shut off all outside air. But since we were here as advisors only, we could carry no weapons. As far as they knew.

That was a sore issue with the pilots. Everyone felt like we should have a weapon there. But the Mexicans were extremely uptight about people having guns. They only let the drug cartels have guns. Once, a pilot was flying to an assignment in Mexico on a regular airline. He hadn't checked his luggage closely and the Mexicans Customs officials found one bullet in a bag. They took him to jail, even though he had a federal agent badge and was coming into the country at their request. It took two days to get him out of jail and then he was kicked out of the country.

I somehow got pulled into this gun issue and ended up in a high-level meeting in Washington, D.C. The National Director of the Customs

Air program called and asked me to attend a meeting with Ray Kelly, who was at the time the under-secretary of the Treasury. US Customs Service was part of the Treasury Department. The director needed an experienced pilot at the meeting in case the under-secretary asked any questions about how things really were in Mexico.

I walked into Kelly's huge office at the Treasury building with the director and right away noticed the view from his large window. There was a magnificent view of the White House! Few people in Washington had a view like this. Without saying a word, it declared to anyone who entered the room, "I am a very important man with very important friends, so beware." It turned out that Mr. Kelly was one of the good guys. I met him again later, after he became the commissioner of customs. He's now the police commissioner in New York City.

He was a busy man, so we got to the point of the meeting in a hurry. Customs had requested that its agents and pilots be allowed to carry weapons while on duty in Mexico. It was going to be a major ordeal to convince the Mexicans to let us do it. So, before Kelly went to the Mexican government with the request, he wanted to know how some of us who had actually worked there felt about it.

He talked awhile about all the legal problems we could have if we had to actually use a weapon in Mexico. All the time he was talking, I was thinking, "You mean he doesn't know we've been taking guns into Mexico the last few months?"

The special agent in charge of the Office of Investigations was also at the meeting, and the way he was talking, he made it sound like the special agents didn't have guns in Mexico. We had been told to keep our weapons out of sight and not to let anyone know we had them. I knew guns were not allowed there, but since they were issued to us for the trip, I figured it was one of those "don't ask, don't tell" things.

We would have been in serious trouble if we had been caught with them, I found out. When Kelly asked me what I thought about having weapons in Mexico, it was hard to keep a straight face. We convinced him to move forward with the request to Mexico. They turned us down. They said it was safe in Mexico. Yeah, right!

For the record, in case there is anything I have said that is not outside the statute of limitations, the only weapons we ever had in

Mexico were for survival purposes only. You know, in case we crash landed and had to shoot a polar bear or something else to eat.

Back to Monterrey. It was a large city surrounded by mountains. It was often foggy there, so when we came in to land sometimes, all we could see were mountain peaks sticking up through a solid white blanket of fog. When we descended into this fog and lost all visibility, it was easy to imagine running into one of those mountains. That was one instrument approach where you really paid attention to what you were doing. A few degrees off course and you were toast.

The only time I ever made a case while flying out of Monterrey was the result of a smuggler's really bad luck. He was driving a load of marijuana up to the border in an old pickup truck. As he was driving across the desert, he got his truck stuck in the sand. The bundles of grass in the back weighed a hundred pounds each. It was hot and there was nothing but rocks, sand, and dirt for twenty miles—so he left them and started walking. I was doing a patrol and spotted the truck in the middle of nowhere. I made a low pass and saw the bales in the back. That was my one and only load of dope seized out of Monterrey, and it was so uneventful that I'm almost ashamed to even mention it.

The landscape in northern Mexico is mostly desert. There were hundreds of square miles of some of the most desolate land I had ever seen, even worse than southern Arizona. In all my flying, I would not see any place as barren and lifeless as this land until I saw Afghanistan. The geography of Afghanistan made northern Mexico look like the Garden of Eden.

An interesting side note about my trips to Monterrey is a couple of things I discovered there. I always like to visit the museums of the places I visit. Monterrey has a great museum, very informative, about the ancient history of Mexico. It had some replicas of several old Mayan cities. I had visited several of these ruins, but I had no idea that there had been so many large cities spread across Mexico and Central America. That civilization was a great deal more advanced than most of the world at its time.

I found a display that had a thousand-year-old statue of what was certainly a Chinese person. To me it helped prove the theory that there was a great deal more traveling and exploring going on in ancient times than we know about. For instance, in the United States, there is lots of evidence that shows that the Egyptians explored America thousands of years before Columbus.

The other interesting discovery was in a cave more than five thousand feet above sea level. It was a tourist attraction, and inside, embedded in the rock walls, were sea shells. It reminded me of when I was growing up in Tennessee, when people would find sea shells while digging water wells. I found that there is evidence all over the world of a flood where the ocean water covered the earth. I guess the story about old Noah was right after all.

On the Citation patrols I flew out of Monterrey, I became very familiar with the Mexican side of the border. Years later, when I was transferred to the Houston Air Branch, this knowledge helped me a good deal. Houston's area of responsibility included the same section of the border, but on the American side. Knowing the lay of the land to the south gave me a better perspective on what we were up against.

After a few trips to Monterrey, the smugglers knew we were there and moved their smuggling routes over to the Yucatan Peninsula. Customs started detailing us to Mérida. They really were getting good at selecting living quarters, and they put us up in another four star hotel. The smugglers' intel was getting a lot better, though, and I never got the chance to chase an airplane there.

I did get to visit some more Mayan ruins and visit a museum that had the largest display of Mayan writing in the world. But as far as chasing bad guys, it wasn't happening, so customs started concentrating on another big problem, illegal immigration.

CHAPTER SEVENTEEN

Undocumented aliens (UDAs) were coming across the border in Arizona by the thousands. US Customs had a big operation there to help the Border Patrol stop this tidal wave of humans seeking a better life in the good old USA. It was called ABCI for Arizona Border Control Initiative. We placed a dozen helicopters and fifty extra pilots from around the nation at the Tucson Air Branch, located on the Davis-Monthan Air Force Base in Tucson.

The operation lasted for three months, and I spent about two months total time there. My usual schedule was a four-hour flight along the border looking for UDAs who had walked across the border. There were very few times that I did not find at least two or three. One time, I found more than a hundred in one group.

There was always a border patrol agent in the helicopter with me who knew the area well. He would call to other BP agents on the ground and tell them where to come and pick up the UDAs we found. The BP agents working on the ground often came across tracks and followed them. Sometimes they would request that the helicopter fly ahead and try to spot the UDAs.

It was just like living the old Wild West days of tracking down Indians. Some of the border patrol agents on the ground were even riding horses. Once I saw a BP agent lasso a UDA from horseback as he was trying to run away.

All the UDAs had this very peculiar habit that was very comical. They must have all gone to the same "sneaking across the border" school. When they heard the helicopter approaching, they would hide under the only cover they could find in the desert, which was usually a small bush about five feet high. The bushes grew as solitary plants, and there was usually only one bush every ten feet or so. The UDAs would try to hide under a bush, but their legs always stuck out. I would be flying along at a very low altitude looking for them and see a bush with about ten legs sticking out from it.

It was kind of like an ostrich sticking its head in the sand and thinking that it was hidden. Even if I hovered right over the top of them they would not move. Most of the time, I would have to land and the border patrol agent would get out and tap them on the legs and tell them to get out of the bush. For some reason, almost all of the UDAs did the same thing.

We would catch a group of UDAs and radio to the border patrol and they would come out in a truck and pick them up. Then we would go catch another group. Sometimes the groups were so large that a bus was required to pick them all up. Other times, the group would be in such a remote area that the Blackhawk had to fly them out to a road where border patrol could collect them.

This went on day after day, week after week. I think that, during the operation, we found more than fifty thousand UDAs. The border patrol would process them and take them back to the border and release them, making sure they crossed back into Mexico. One border patrol agent told me that he had picked up the same person sixteen different times.

In July and August, the temperatures would reach over 115°. The operation would turn from a search mission to a rescue mission. The UDAs, including women and children, would attempt to cross the desert in this hot temperature with only one bottle of water apiece. Sometimes they would have to walk as much as fifty miles before they had arranged for someone to pick them up along a highway.

Needless to say, they were often in very bad shape when we found them. We would medevac them to a hospital or an aid station if required. Often, we just found bodies. There were even times when the UDAs called border patrol on their cell phones and pleaded for someone to come and get them. I often flew long hours searching for these callers because they did not know exactly where they were.

At night, we would get a customs airplane to fly overhead, searching for hot spots with the infrared camera. The UDAs would sometimes make a campfire at night, which could easily be seen from the airplane. The airplane pilot would radio me in the helicopter and give me a latitude and longitude to go and pick up the UDAs. At night, as I was flying with night vision goggles, the airplane would shoot down a laser beam to the area where they saw the hot spot and I would simply fly to the beam of light.

This laser could only be seen with night vision goggles. It was a narrow beam of greenish light that seemingly came out of the sky like some kind of alien death ray. It was an amazing sight to see. If you followed the beam up with your eyes to where it originated in the sky, it seemed to come from a glowing circular disk. If I didn't know better, I would swear that it was coming from a UFO. It is probably a good thing that the UDAs could not see this beam of light or they would still be running.

One day, I was flying the AStar helicopter during the day and I noticed a large dust cloud about three miles in front of me. I assumed this was a large group of the illegal immigrants walking across the desert. When I arrived at the spot, there was a small ravine. Down in the ravine was the second-largest longhorn steer I had ever seen. I bet it weighed a ton. It was scratching its back against the bank and stirring up quite a dust storm. I guess the steers were running wild out there. I was glad that I was in the helicopter and not down in that ditch with another longhorn steer. I had already done that once, and once was enough.

I would often find abandoned vehicles in the desert. The UDAs would steal them in Mexico and use them to cross the border. They would drive northbound through the desert as far as they could—until they ran out of gas or it became impassable. Then they abandoned them. We averaged finding about two vehicles every day.

Sometimes the UDAs crossing the border would be carrying backpacks filled with illegal drugs. They were a little harder to catch, because they would not stop running as long as they thought they had a chance to get away. They were also the dangerous ones, because sometimes they had weapons.

There were also bandits in the area who would rob the UDAs of what little money they had. They knew that the UDAs would not report them. I felt bad for some of these people, especially the older ones and the women and children.

Their lives in Mexico must have been really terrible if they were willing to risk their lives to get into America. Most were just average people searching for a better way of life. If I had been in their shoes, I would probably be doing the same thing. But I didn't establish our immigration policy or write our immigration laws. I was just the one that was hired to enforce them.

But not all of the UDAs were nice people. Some were thieves and killers who were coming to America with criminal intent. Some came here not to work, but to rob and plunder. From the air, you could not tell the good from the bad, so we arrested them all.

The ABCI operation was definitely an eye-opener for me. I never realized how open our border was or that there were so many people coming across it. Maybe America wasn't as screwed up as everyone in the world seemed to claim it was. If it was, wouldn't there be thousands of people leaving instead of trying to get in?

It was my day off when I saw on live TV a jet airliner crash into the World Trade Center. I recalled the time when I had stood between those buildings and marveled at what man can build. This event led to a lot of changes within the US Customs Service. But I'll talk about that in a minute. First, let me tell you about the role customs aviation played those first few days.

Like I said, I was off that day. I called the office, anticipating that all the pilots would be needed in some capacity. I found out that almost every aircraft in the whole country had been grounded. The only airplanes flying in the United States were a few military fighters and Air Force One.

It was far too soon to have a game plan. As far as customs could determine, there was little that we could do at the moment. A few hours later the New Orleans Air Branch got its first mission. The president was flying into Barksdale Air Force Base in Shreveport, Louisiana. The secret service wanted to get two agents up there from the New Orleans office ASAP. We coordinated with the National Command Center for permission to make the flight and the Citation was soon airborne. We were among only a handful of people in the world who knew where the president was heading.

Air Force One landed about forty-five minutes ahead of the Citation. The pilot flying the Citation told me that as he radioed to Barksdale AFB for landing instructions, a stern voice came over the radio and asked just who exactly he was and why he was landing in Barksdale. The pilot answered with, "Just who are you and why are you on this radio?" The voice replied, "This is Air Force One!"

Well, I think you can guess who won that debate. It turned out that the secret service had suspected that there might be an attempt to crash a plane into Air Force One. They had routed all radar and communications to them in the plane and were carefully watching all aircraft anywhere around. Our Citation was the only airplane south of Washington, D.C., that was in the air.

That was the only flight that first day. The second day, we were asked to pick up some aviation experts and fly them to Washington, D.C. to check the crash site at the Pentagon. After that, we got another mission to fly some VIPs to New York City. Customs and the military were still the only organizations allowed to fly in the entire United States.

Of course, that couldn't last forever, and after things settled down a little bit, aircraft were allowed to fly again, with certain restrictions. One of the new rules was that every aircraft had to be assigned a transponder code coming into the country. This is a code that radar can use to identify aircraft, but I've already told you that in the beginning of this book. You did remember, didn't you?

I was on alert in the Citation, and we got a call to intercept an unknown target coming into southern Louisiana from the Gulf of Mexico. We were in the air in five minutes, flying at max speed to intercept. I noticed an F-15 taking off right behind me. They must have also been scrambled.

When my crew and I finally had a chance to determine exactly where the target had crossed into the United States, we pretty much knew what this target was going to be. I had chased aircraft in that same location a dozen times. An offshore oil rig charter company had a helicopter landing pad there, and it was common for those helicopters to come back from the oil rigs and forget to turn on their transponder.

I intercepted the target just as it was landing. It was just exactly what I knew it would be: an oil rig helicopter. Suddenly a strange voice came over our secure customs radio frequency. It was English, but with a heavy accent. I didn't recognize the nationality. What was this all about?

The voice told me to move away from the target, that the F-15 was going to make the ID. You have to remember that the whole nation was jumpy at that time and the fighters flying over our cities in America were prepared to shoot down any unknown targets.

I knew this target was not a terrorist, and I was about to advise our customs controller of this fact when I received this strange radio call. Now we don't take commands from someone we can't identify, especially in the middle of an intercept with an F-15 closing in.

I called our controller, and once again, the strange voice came on the same frequency, before the customs controller could answer. I'd had enough of this, so I asked the voice to identify itself. There was a long pause. Then the person answered with a military call sign I had never heard of. We were not getting anywhere with this conversation. Then the F-15 passed in front of me, heading straight for the target.

Maybe the F-15 was monitoring this frequency also. I gave the pilot a call and he answered quickly. I explained who the target was and that it was common for it to land here. We both flew over the helipad and the rotors from the target helicopter were already spinning down. I told the F-15 that we would call the charter company and see why they had not had their transponder on. We both determined that this was a non-event and that we were going to return to base.

After I landed, I made some phone calls and found out that the mysterious voice was from a Canadian Air Force AWAC airplane. The United States government had let an aircraft from another country's air force fly in our sovereign airspace to assist us in securing our borders! The arrangement was so secret that not even customs, which was tasked with doing the job, knew they were there.

That is just one example of many knee-jerk reactions that we all went through those first few weeks after 9/11. But in defense of the decision makers, I'm sure they were all doing what they thought was the right thing to do. We had been attacked on American soil in a big way, and there were a lot of unknown factors out there. We were doing all we could do to make sure it didn't happen again, and no one was taking any chances.

The decision was made in Washington, D.C. that in order to make America safer, the government would combine twenty-two federal agencies into one. They called it The US Department of Homeland Security (DHS). The US Customs Service now became US Customs and Border Protection, and it fell within this new Department of Homeland Security.

Shortly afterward, all customs and border patrol aircraft and maritime vessels were combined and became the Office of Air and Marine, the largest law enforcement aviation and maritime organization in the world. Customs pilots and border patrol pilots were now called CBP pilots. Later, our official title became air interdiction agent. The boat pilots became marine interdiction agents. Together we had more than three hundred aircraft and two hundred boats protecting our homeland.

The drug war became the war on terrorism. Our main focus was to prevent another attack. It wasn't long until we realized that both these "wars" were one and the same. We found that almost half of the drug money was directly linked to funding some terrorist organization. As far as CBP Air and Marine was concerned, our mission changed little. We arrested every smuggler we could. It didn't matter if they were smuggling drugs or bombs into the country; both brought death and destruction.

Tom Ridge was named the first secretary of homeland security, and it wasn't long before I was assigned to fly him. It turned out to be a very funny story. As you recall, DHS came up with a color-code system to help warn the public of impending terrorist attacks. Code red was the highest level, and in those first couple of years after 9/11, we went to red quite often. On one such occasion, I was given twenty-four hours to get to Washington, D.C. to assist on a special project. When I arrived in D.C., I discovered that I was on standby to fly Tom Ridge to an "undisclosed location."

I was assigned the AStar helicopter and I stood-by on a twelve-hour shift for ten days at the Reagan National Airport. The first day, I made a practice run, learning where to pick him up and where the "undisclosed location" actually was. It was located in … ha, you didn't think I was going to tell you did you? If I did, I would have to shoot you.

On my twelve-hour shift, I had to be ready to be airborne in less than eight minutes. It takes five minutes to start the helicopter and get the rotor up to flying speed, which meant I had to be sitting in the helicopter in three. I didn't mind being on this high state of readiness because I knew that if I was called, it meant that Washington was under attack. Getting key government officials out of harm's way would be critical to maintaining our government's operations. My only question was, of all the CBP pilots in the country, why did they have to pick me?

One morning, I was in our office, which was inside the hangar. The helicopter was ready to fly, just outside the door. I was rehearsing in my mind my plan of action if I got the call to launch. I was excited to be a part of such an important operation. I turned on the news and there was Tom Ridge, live on TV.

I turned up the volume to hear what he was saying. Then I read the subtitles. He was in Jacksonville, Florida! Here I was on high alert, and he wasn't even in Washington! I guess I wasn't as important as I thought I was.

Up until that point, I had viewed myself as a giant eagle soaring above Washington. I felt as if I could look down with my eagle eyes and actually catch an occasional glimpse of the "big picture." But now, I suddenly realized I wasn't an all-seeing eagle but a tiny white mouse lost in a maze, and I could only see a few steps ahead.

And so I learned to embrace the world of highly classified operations. It is a world where everything is compartmentalized, a world where even the key players are purposely shown only a small piece of the big picture. I had a security clearance high enough to wear a weapon while standing beside the president of the United States, yet I was often left in the dark. They call it "need to know." It doesn't matter how high your security clearance is, if you don't have a "need to know," then you never know.

I guess being the one responsible for flying the secretary of homeland security to a safe place in the event of an emergency didn't rate as a "need to know" about his whereabouts. So be it. I guessed that they didn't need to know where I would be the rest of the day either.

There is one thing I have learned in my years of working for the government. The government is not buildings, or departments, or agencies. The government is really people, and people make mistakes. You can use me as an example. Throughout my twenty-three years of service, I made about every mistake a person could make. Yet somehow, through it all, I managed to get the job done. So don't be too hard on your government. Just ask yourself, could you have done any better?

The New Orleans Air and Marine Branch moved off the Belle Chasse Navy Base to a new hurricane-proof building on the north shore of Lake Pontchartrain in a town called Hammond, Louisiana. And it did so not a moment too soon. Hurricane Katrina struck New Orleans and, well, you've seen the pictures. Actually, I had gotten out of New Orleans at the right time, also. I had been promoted to supervisor and had taken a position at the Houston Air and Marine Branch. I moved four months before Katrina hit.

The New Orleans Air Branch was in a perfect location to help support FEMA and a lot of other federal, state, and local organizations. The Air Branch had this big new hangar and better yet, a large generator that could power everything the branch needed. Electric power was off for hundreds of square miles, so the branch became the command center for all federal air support operations.

One interesting flight did happen during the relief operation. Some of the citizens in New Orleans decided that, with all the chaos going on, it was a good time to start looting the city. For several days, there was almost complete lawlessness. Businesses and homes were being robbed, people were being murdered. It was out of control. We even had to supply the New Orleans police department with ammunition. It was a war zone in some areas.

Finally, the NOPD requested federal help and CBP responded with the largest law enforcement helicopter assault in US history. We loaded four Blackhawk helicopters with the best special response teams from around the country. Then we flew in and landed on a street in downtown New Orleans. The teams assisted NOPD, along with other law enforcement organizations, and finally secured the city.

Only a couple of years later, Hurricane Ike hit Houston and the Texas coastline. The citizens there were a little more civilized, and there were none of the New Orleans-type problems. There was, however, a great deal of property damage along the beaches south of Houston. I made a helicopter flight soon after the hurricane struck and saw a ten mile-long line of timber and debris, about a mile inland, that had once been beautiful homes on the beach.

The Houston Air and Marine Branch became much like Hammond had become during Katina—the center for the federal aviation response. We had numerous helicopters and airplanes from around the country at the branch to support FEMA and anyone else who needed aviation support. CBP Air and Marine was now recognized not only as the agency that protected our borders, but also as the air force for FEMA and any other national homeland security emergency.

While I was a supervisor in Houston, I had the opportunity to work with the Port Isabel Marine Unit for six weeks. This unit was located at the southernmost port of the barrier islands along the Texas coastline, just a few miles from where the Rio Grande River enters the Gulf of Mexico. There were lots of boats coming out of Mexico and smuggling their dope into the remote parts of these islands.

I haven't really given the marine part of the Office of Air and Marine a lot of attention in this book because I was mostly an airplane driver. But let me tell you, after spending six weeks with the boat drivers, I know that they are every bit the highly trained professionals, just like the airplane pilots. Believe me that chasing a smuggling vessel through four-foot seas at night going seventy miles an hour takes a great deal of skill. CBP has some very fast boat interceptors, and I got to drive them in high-speed chases (during training) on calm seas and under sunny skies. I have a great deal of respect for the boat guys who go out on cold, dark nights, in stormy seas, to protect our coastline. I wouldn't want to do it!

Several of the marine interdiction agents at Port Isabel had transferred over from the border patrol. They had patrolled the Rio Grande River in small boats, which I think is perhaps the most dangerous job in CBP. The Rio Grande is a very narrow river, and they told me many stories about being shot at from the Mexican side. Patrolling that river at night had to be very scary.

I spent five years as a supervisor in Houston and continued to fly the Citation and the AStar helicopter. I spent time as the deputy director and later the acting director for the Houston Air and Marine Branch. As acting director, I was responsible for the CBP air and marine assets for the entire Texas coastline. I had definitely come a long way from when I first walked into the New Orleans Air Branch over two decades earlier.

I was facing mandatory retirement age, so it was time to turn things over to the next group of young pilots. We had a new man in charge of the aviation program in Washington, and he had big and exciting plans to expand the Office of Air and Marine. Homeland Security had finally recognized the important role of the Office of Air and Marine, and now our national director was elevated to the assistant commissioner level. He had helped transform the rag-tag, blue-jean-wearing group of cowboys we once were into the largest and most professional law enforcement air and marine organization in the world. The whole upper management team in D.C. was now very experienced and competent. I was confident that the Office of Air and Marine was in good hands and would get along just fine without me.

In 2009, I retired and thought my aviation adventures had come to an end. Little did I know that I would soon be having some of my greatest adventures of all! I was hired as a government contract pilot to fly US army spy planes in Iraq and Afghanistan. I would end up flying sixty-one combat missions. But that's another story.

In the twenty-three years I spent flying with Homeland Security and legacy US Customs, I flew state-of-the-art aircraft throughout the United States and in over a dozen countries. I have flown over oceans, mountains, jungles, and deserts. I have met three presidents, and several senators, governors, and other VIPs. But the most rewarding part of my career was having worked with the most dedicated, professional, and intelligent people in the world: all the people of the Office of Air and Marine. It was a great ride!

THE END